CAMPAIGN 392

EARLY PACIFIC RAIDS 1942

The American Carriers Strike Back

BRIAN LANE HERDER

ILLUSTRATED BY ADAM TOOBY

Series editor Nikolai Bogdanovic

OSPREY PUBLISHING
Bloomsbury Publishing Plc
Kemp House, Chawley Park, Cumnor Hill, Oxford OX2 9PH, UK
29 Earlsfort Terrace, Dublin 2, Ireland
1385 Broadway, 5th Floor, New York, NY 10018, USA
E-mail: info@ospreypublishing.com
www.ospreypublishing.com

OSPREY is a trademark of Osprey Publishing Ltd

First published in Great Britain in 2023

A catalog record for this book is available from the British Library.

ISBN: PB 9781472854872; eBook 9781472854889;
ePDF 9781472854896; XML 9781472854902

23 24 25 26 27   10 9 8 7 6 5 4 3 2 1

Maps by Bounford.com
3D BEVs by Paul Kime
Index by Fionbar Lyons
Typeset by PDQ Digital Media Solutions, Bungay, UK
Printed and bound in India by Replika Press Private Ltd.

Osprey Publishing supports the Woodland Trust, the UK's leading woodland
conservation charity.

To find out more about our authors and books visit
www.ospreypublishing.com. Here you will find extracts, author
interviews, details of forthcoming events and the option to sign up for
our newsletter.

Artist's note

Readers can find out more about the work of battlescene illustrator Adam
Tooby by visiting the following website:

www.adamtooby.com

Author's note

Times and dates given are local, unless otherwise stated.

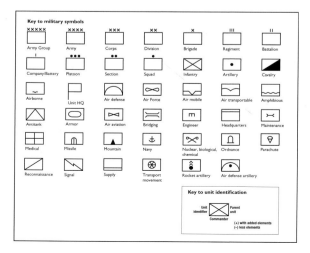

Front cover main illustration: *Yokohama Maru* comes under TBD
Devastator attack at Salamaua, 10 March 1942. (Adam Tooby)

Title page photograph: An SBD Dauntless of either VB-6 or VS-6
prepares to launch from *Enterprise* for a target in the Marshalls on
February 1, 1942. (NNAM.1996.253.599)

CONTENTS

ORIGINS OF THE CAMPAIGN

After the devastating Japanese blows of December 1941, the Allies found themselves reeling with defeat everywhere in the Pacific. Nonetheless, and despite being outnumbered 11:4 in battleships and 10:3 in carriers, the US Navy's new commander-in-chief Admiral Ernest J. King vowed to hit back at Japan's rapidly expanding Pacific empire immediately.

The resulting American naval raids were the first-ever combat actions of US aircraft carriers, an as yet unproven weapon system that would ultimately dominate the Pacific War. King's Pacific Fleet carriers were organized into three small task forces of one carrier and about two cruisers and five to six destroyers each. Between February 1 and March 10, 1942, these three small task forces launched several unexpected raids throughout the Japanese defensive perimeter in the Central and South Pacific, which often included US cruisers and destroyers closing to shell the enemy islands and sweep Japanese shipping and escorts.

Utilizing high-speed "hit-and-run" tactics to keep the Japanese off balance, the early 1942 US naval raids are badly under-reported in standard Pacific War histories. As a later foreword to an Office of Naval Intelligence narrative explained, "Not one battlewagon engaged in any of these raids, which were combination carrier attacks and bombardments. Carriers began to show their beyond-the-horizon capabilities, and cruisers provided the biggest guns." As the first tentative Allied counterattacks of the Pacific War, these episodes illustrate the US Navy during a fleetingly rare 20th-century position of severe and widespread American military inferiority.

No work this size could hope to address all Pacific War operations of early 1942. Instead, this book will address these early 1942 US naval raids, along with the Japanese Pacific operations that precipitated and followed them.

An *Enterprise* TBD soars over a burning Wake Island, February 24, 1942. The USN's early Pacific raids saw the first World War II combat actions of many relatively junior US admirals, naval officers, and naval aviators who would ultimately become much more famous, such as Bill Halsey, Raymond Spruance, Frank Jack Fletcher, Thomas Kinkaid, Frederick C. "Ted" Sherman, J.J. "Jocko" Clark, Jimmy Thach, and Butch O'Hare, among others. (NHHC 80-CF-1071-1)

PEARL HARBOR AND AFTERMATH, DECEMBER 7–10, 1941

The IJN's December 7, 1941 surprise raid on Pearl Harbor has been heavily documented and needs little special elaboration here. However, some background is relevant to explaining the future 1942 campaign. Japan's unlikely strategy to pre-emptively hammer Pearl Harbor with all six IJN fleet carriers was rammed through by Combined Fleet commander Admiral Isoroku Yamamoto, with the attack itself planned by Yamamoto's brilliant operational tactician, career aviator Commander Minoru Genda. Commanding Kido Butai (the actual IJN carrier task force itself) was Vice Admiral Chuichi Nagumo.

At no point did Yamamoto believe that any amount of material destruction wrought on Pearl Harbor could militarily win the war for Japan. Instead, Yamamoto hoped to so demoralize the American public in the war's first few hours that the United States would shortly give up. The objective was therefore not to destroy US naval might, but to destroy American morale. Although Yamamoto himself personally believed battleships were obsolete, battleships had long been considered the traditional symbols of modern naval power. The US battleship force was therefore Yamamoto's main target at Pearl Harbor.

However, the IJN's archconservative but supine Naval General Staff (NGS) officially outranked Yamamoto. The NGS reluctantly acquiesced to Yamamoto's risky Pearl Harbor scheme only on the condition that Kido Butai's survival was paramount. They therefore dictated that Kido Butai's top priority would not be the Pacific Fleet battleships, but Oahu's land-based air strength. Yamamoto officially agreed to this condition, then promptly disobeyed, secretly reminding Nagumo and Genda that the strike's priority was the US battle line, as destroying American morale was the whole point of the exercise. Genda formally agreed with Yamamoto that the US battleships were the main target, before himself secretly informing his approving carrier air groups that the main targets at Pearl Harbor were not Yamamoto's obsolescent battleships, but Kido Butai's own American counterpart, the Pacific Fleet carriers.

However, to Genda's dismay, preliminary Japanese reconnaissance found no US carriers at Hawaii on the morning of December 7. Nevertheless, two waves totaling 353 Japanese carrier aircraft began attacking the Pearl Harbor base complex on Oahu at 0748hrs local time. Of the eight US battleships present, two were destroyed, two settled in shallow water, and the remainder received various degrees of damage. An additional three cruisers, three destroyers, and five auxiliaries were damaged, and a training ship was sunk. Of 402 total US aircraft, 188 were destroyed and 159 damaged, almost all on the ground. By the time the

Battleship *Arizona* explodes in the first few minutes of the Pearl Harbor attack on the morning of December 7, 1941. This image is a still frame from a color film being shot that morning. *Arizona's* catastrophic demise not only killed 1,177 men nearly instantly, it also symbolized the immediate destruction of all prewar US Navy plans to fight the Japanese. (NHHC 80-G-K-13512)

Rear Admiral Spruance's flagship, heavy cruiser *Northampton*, steams into Pearl Harbor on December 8, 1941. She is accompanied by the rest of Vice Admiral Bill Halsey's Task Force 8. After viewing the wreckage from the treacherous attack, Halsey famously declared that when he was done with them, "the only place Japanese will be spoken is in hell." (NHHC 80-G-32548)

last Japanese plane departed, total American casualties were 2,403 killed and 1,178 wounded, compared to Japanese losses of just 29 planes and five midget submarines. Yet the Americans' defeat could have been much worse. In fact, shocked and despondent US officials legitimately feared Hawaii would be invaded. Indeed, this had been Genda's original plan before superiors had vetoed it. Additionally, and again despite Genda's original plan, Pearl Harbor's repair and logistic facilities had ultimately been deemed lower priority targets, and as the sun fell on December 7, they remained almost entirely intact.

All three Pacific Fleet carrier task forces were famously absent from Pearl Harbor on December 7. *Saratoga* and her task force, commanded by Rear Admiral Aubrey W. Fitch, was still at San Diego. *Saratoga* would depart California the morning of December 8, as originally scheduled, and reach Pearl Harbor on December 15. Temporarily commanded by Rear Admiral John H. Newton, Task Force 12 consisted of carrier *Lexington*, heavy cruisers *Astoria*, *Portland*, and *Chicago*, and five destroyers. The morning of December 7, TF-12 was 420nm southeast of Midway Island and scheduled to fly off VMA-231 at 1200hrs to reinforce the Midway garrison; TF-12's permanent commander, Vice Admiral Wilson Brown, was temporarily detached on exercises in heavy cruiser *Indianapolis*. Vice Admiral Bill Halsey's Task Force 8, centered around *Enterprise*, was returning from a similar fighter reinforcement of Wake Island and was just 200nm west of Pearl Harbor during the attack; *Enterprise* lost ten planes shot down over Oahu by Japanese fighters and American antiaircraft fire. Over the next several days attempts were made to find and pursue Nagumo's withdrawing Kido Butai, but fortunately for the Americans the US carriers never found them.

Back at Pearl Harbor, shaken Pacific Fleet staff issued a situation report on December 10:

With the losses we have sustained, it is necessary to revise completely our strategy of a Pacific war. The loss of battleships commits us to the strategic defensive until our forces can again be built up. However, a very powerful striking force of carriers, cruisers, and destroyers survives. These forces must be operated boldly and vigorously on the tactical offensive in order to retrieve our initial disaster.

The report recommended the following courses of action:

1.   Employ three search-strike carrier groups, of which two will be constantly at sea and third replenishing at Pearl, to intercept enemy raids and support menaced bases.

2.   Organize battleships and destroyer types in escort groups for coast-to-islands convoy operations. Base the battleships at San Francisco to relieve congestion at Pearl; they will be relieved by Pearl-based cruiser and destroyer escort groups at a mid-ocean meeting point not far from the islands.

3.   Strip the West Coast of all but local defense forces, which may be used as escorts for coastal convoys.

4. Employ submarines offensively in Japanese waters, and off Wake and Midway.

5. Organize a thorough offshore search with Army bombers and Navy patrol planes.

6. Keep Australia-bound shipping to the minimum for which escorts are available

7. Encourage and assist the Army to build up land-based pursuit and bomber strength on Oahu as rapidly as possible, and to establish a proper antiaircraft defense of Pearl Harbor. A vast augmentation of ship and shore radar installations will be vitally necessary.

However, Hawaiian waters still teemed with IJN submarines. As of late December 7, Rear Admiral Shigeteru Yamazaki's 2nd Submarine Squadron had deployed seven I-boats east of Oahu while Rear Admiral Shigeyoshi Miwa's 3rd Submarine Squadron had nine I-boats south of the island. An additional five I-boats under Captain Hankyu Sasaki were also on station, having carried midget subs to the Pearl Harbor attack.

On December 7–8, I-69 was nearly sunk by US destroyers and a minefield off Hawaii but escaped. Early the following morning, I-6 sighted and unsuccessfully attacked *Enterprise* off Kauai. *Enterprise* was subsequently pursued by multiple Truk-based I-boats over the next two days and unsuccessfully fired upon. However, early on December 10 an *Enterprise* SBD sighted and disabled the surfaced *I-70*. Several hours later a second SBD sent *I-70* to the bottom without survivors, making *I-70* the first IJN warship lost to US aircraft in World War II. The initial Japanese submarine blockade of Hawaii would ultimately claim just five merchantmen by its end on December 23.

The Pacific Fleet's future 1941 commander, Admiral Husband E. Kimmel, is viewed in 1939 as a cruiser division commander. Although caught off-guard at Pearl Harbor, Kimmel was an overall heady and aggressive officer. He would be denied any chance to retaliate against the Japanese and would be unfairly scapegoated for the Pearl Harbor disaster. (NHHC NH 50266)

FAILED WAKE ISLAND RELIEF, DECEMBER 14–23

Annexed by the United States in 1899, lonely Wake Atoll lay 1,025nm southwest of US-occupied Midway Island and 1,300nm northeast of Guam, but a mere 450nm north of Bikini in the Japanese-occupied Marshall Islands and just 620nm from the Marshalls' main Japanese airbase at Kwajalein. In 1940 Congress had belatedly authorized the USN to transform Wake into a forward air and submarine base. Like Guam and the Philippines, Wake had always been an obvious Japanese target and horribly exposed, but in early 1941 the US Pacific Fleet commander, Admiral Husband Kimmel, had recognized Japan's anticipated wartime invasion of Wake as an "opportunity to get at naval forces with naval forces. We should try by every possible means to get the Japanese to expose naval units."

The morning of Pearl Harbor (December 8 local time), the US garrison on Wake Island comprised 542 US military personnel and 1,216 American civilians, plus 12 obsolescent F4F-3 Wildcat fighters. IJN medium bombers from Kwajalein hammered Wake on December 8–9. The first, poorly planned Japanese landing on Wake was attempted in the early dark of December 11 (local time). By mid-morning the beleaguered USMC garrison had heroically

Wake's Peale Island and lagoon viewed in May 1941. The prewar Wake was a major stopover point for Pan Am airlines' trans-Pacific seaplane service. A Pan Am seaplane is visible along with seven Navy PBY patrol planes. Also visible is the Pan Am base at the seaplane pier. (NHHC 80-G-451194)

Frank Jack Fletcher photographed as a vice admiral, mid-war. Fletcher's reputation is almost inexplicably complicated, although the man himself was simple and straightforward. Modern naval historians have only just recently begun to rehabilitate Fletcher's complex legacy. (NHHC NH 91214)

sunk two IJN destroyers and repulsed the invasion, a unique Pacific War accomplishment that embarrassed the IJN. There was no doubt, however, that the Japanese would be back in force.

Kimmel's two major mid-1941 war plans, *WPUSF-44* and *WPPac-46*, had both included a diversionary scheme for two widely separated US carrier task forces to raid the Marshall Islands. This "Marshalls Reconnaissance and Raiding Plan" was now adapted into a complex scheme to relieve the Wake garrison. The plan involved all three available carrier task forces, but they were to be widely separated for diversionary purposes. Vice Admiral Wilson Brown's *Lexington* task group (now renamed TF-11) was to launch a diversionary attack against Jaluit, while Vice Admiral Bill Halsey's *Enterprise* task group (TF-8) functioned as a distant reserve.

The actual counteroffensive against Wake itself was delegated to Rear Admiral Aubrey Fitch's cobbled-together *Saratoga* task force, TF-14. In addition to her own planes, *Saratoga* carried VMF-221, the USMC fighter squadron (18 Brewster F2A Buffaloes) intended to reinforce the beleaguered island's defenses. Accompanying TF-14 was seaplane tender *Tangier* (AV-8), carrying a detachment of the 4th Marine Battalion as well as stores and ammunition for Wake. In a worst-case scenario Wake's entire garrison was to be evacuated aboard *Tangier*, a theoretical and dubious prospect.

Almost immediately, however, the Americans' overly complicated Wake relief plan began to devolve into a tragic farce. The first and most significant problem was the Wake mission's muddled goals: to reinforce the marine garrison *at* Wake, to evacuate the marine garrison *from* Wake, and/or to ambush the IJN fleet *off* Wake. Exactly which objective was intended to be the primary mission has not been satisfactorily resolved 80 years later.

This crisis was compounded by command problems. The only possible heavy cruisers available to escort *Saratoga* were *Astoria*, *Minneapolis*, and *San Francisco* of Rear Admiral Frank Jack Fletcher's Cruiser Division Six. Unlike Fitch, Fletcher was not an experienced aviator, but he was very slightly senior to Fitch in rank. Following standard naval protocol, Kimmel assigned overall command to Fletcher, who did not logically transfer to carrier *Saratoga* but retained his flag aboard cruiser *Astoria*. After numerous delays TF-14 departed Pearl Harbor on December 15.

Then, on December 17, the disgraced Kimmel was suddenly removed from Pacific Fleet command and temporarily replaced with Vice Admiral William Pye as interim commander. Pye had been Kimmel's Battle Force commander, but Pye lacked Kimmel's natural aggression and decisiveness. Pye further complicated matters by simultaneously consulting both his own Battle Force staff and Kimmel's Pacific Fleet staff. More reasonably, Pye also understood that he was merely a placeholder commander, and he was understandably reluctant to expose his successor's Pacific Fleet carriers to superior Japanese airpower.

Vice Admiral William S. Pye in late 1941 or early 1942. Pye was the Pacific Fleet Battle Force (battleships) commander. He was particularly risk-averse, a characteristic not uncommon in the unusually conservative "Gun Club" of traditional battleship officers. (NHHC NH 82801)

Meanwhile, en route to strike Jaluit, on December 18 Brown received a paranoid report that the IJN had reinforced the area with a large submarine force and up to 200 planes. The afternoon of December 20, Pye ordered Brown north instead, to directly assist *Saratoga* at Wake with *Lexington*. Meanwhile Halsey's *Enterprise* had put into Pearl on December 16 to replenish, before sortieing from Hawaii on December 20 for the assigned reserve position 100nm west of Midway.

Already burdened by radio silence and his oiler's 13-knot top speed, Fletcher had been required by Kimmel to refuel at a prearranged rendezvous point in case *Lexington* appeared. Then, late on December 22, sudden high winds and seas dragged Fletcher's refueling out to a maddening ten hours, during which TF-14 made virtually no headway towards Wake. Such unforeseen operational problems, from the trivial to the momentous, increasingly stacked up. It was becoming painfully apparent that the Pacific Fleet's carrier task forces were still unprepared to operate under wartime conditions.

By now the IJN's second Wake invasion fleet had been reinforced to six heavy cruisers, light cruiser *Yubari*, old light cruisers *Tatsuta* and *Tenryu*, seven destroyers, seaplane tender *Kiyokawa*, minelayer *Tsugaru*, two fast transports, and three auxiliary transports. Providing heavy air support were detached fleet carriers *Soryu* and *Hiryu*, two heavy cruisers, and two destroyers. In the meantime Wake had been getting pounded daily by medium bombers from the Marshalls. Then, on December 21 (East longitude date), *Soryu* and *Hiryu* launched their first strikes against Wake from a point 200nm northwest of the island. *Saratoga* had only 77 flyable aircraft (26 fighters) compared to *Soryu* and *Hiryu*'s combined 94 planes (34 fighters). This force disparity was accurately read by Pacific Fleet intelligence at Pearl Harbor.

After several days of aerial pounding, the 2nd Maizuru Special Naval Landing Force (SNLF) assaulted Wake early on December 23 and began to overrun the island against fierce but hopeless US resistance. *Saratoga* was still 420nm from Wake. After five hours of agonizing debate back at Pearl Harbor, at 0755hrs Pye ordered Fletcher to retire, essentially abandoning the marines to their fate. As one US admiral succinctly put it: "Wake is now and will continue to be a liability."

Upon receiving Pye's order to withdraw, an irate Fletcher tore his cap off and slammed it onto the deck. Aboard *Saratoga*, Fitch felt his subordinate officers' talk was becoming borderline mutinous, and he discreetly excused himself from *Saratoga*'s bridge. Finally, at 1630hrs, nearly three hours after the Wake garrison was forced to surrender, a reluctant Fletcher duly complied and turned TF-14 back towards Pearl Harbor. One of Fletcher's cruiser skippers admonished, "Frank Jack should have placed the telescope to his blind eye like Nelson." A *Saratoga* war diary complained, "Everyone seems to feel that it's the war between the two yellow races." Nevertheless, some were willing to consider a wider view. A *Saratoga* fighter pilot admitted to his diary: "The set up seemed perfect for those of us who did not have the complete picture of the strategical situation."

YAMAMOTO'S SUBMARINE OFFENSIVE AGAINST HAWAII AND THE US WEST COAST, DECEMBER 1941

On December 7, the IJN's Expeditionary Force of 20 large, long-range submarines had been deployed in an aggressive blockade off Oahu ranging from 8.5nm to 100nm south of Pearl Harbor. These so-called I-boats utterly failed to contribute substantially to the Pearl Harbor raid. However, within minutes of the Pearl Harbor strike, *I-26* attacked and sank the US Army-chartered 2,140-ton steam schooner *Cynthia Olson* some 300nm west of San Francisco.

Yamamoto was painfully aware he had missed the US carriers at Pearl Harbor. However, he wrongly assumed the Pacific Fleet carriers would not immediately return to operate out of Hawaii, speculating they would redeploy either to Australia or to the US West Coast. To Yamamoto the most obvious US ports for the Pacific Fleet carriers were the major US naval bases at San Diego and San Francisco, Puget Sound Navy Yard in Bremerton, Washington state, and the Columbia River shipyards in the states

Japanese submarine *I-26* viewed cruising in Hiroshima Bay, October 1941. *I-26* was a Type B1 submarine. When surfaced, she had a top speed of 23.5 knots and displaced 2,584 tons. With her long range she was sent to the US West Coast shortly after Pearl Harbor. (Public Domain)

of Washington and Oregon. Therefore, shortly after December 7 Yamamoto ordered a major submarine blockade of the US West Coast to find and sink the elusive US carriers. As a secondary mission, Yamamoto additionally ordered each Japanese submarine to surface and fire 30 shells at American shore targets the night of Christmas Eve. As Christmas 1941 approached, a total of nine Japanese submarines had deployed off every major US West Coast port between Canada's Vancouver Island and the California border with Mexico: *I-9*, *I-10*, *I-15*, *I-17*, *I-19*, *I-21*, *I-23*, *I-25*, and *I-26*.

However, by December 22, Yamamoto mistakenly believed the US Atlantic Fleet battleships *Mississippi*, *New Mexico*, and *Idaho* were due to arrive in Los Angeles on Christmas Day. Yamamoto now ordered his submarines to sink the phantom US battleships, postponing his originally scheduled Christmas Eve shellings to December 27. Rear Admiral Tsutomu Sato duly ordered *I-17*, *I-25*, and his own flagship *I-9* to intercept the US battleships. However, dangerously low fuel and unexpectedly aggressive US anti-submarine patrols inspired Sato to cancel all West Coast operations on December 27 and withdraw. By mid-January even the remaining I-boats off Hawaii would return to Kwajalein, ending the IJN's uninspired eastern Pacific blockade.

REFORMING THE US PACIFIC FLEET 1941–42

The Pearl Harbor disaster demanded an immediate shakeup in the USN's top fleet commands. The new Commander-in-Chief, US Fleet (COMINCH) would be Admiral Ernest J. King, who would direct the naval war from Washington, DC. On December 24, 1941 King issued his first announcement as impending COMINCH: "The way to victory is long. The going will be hard. We will do the best we can with what we've got. We must have more planes and ships—at once. Then it will be our turn to strike. We will win through—in time."

Replacing Kimmel as US Pacific Fleet commander was Admiral Chester Nimitz, who arrived at Pearl Harbor on December 25. To everyone's surprise, Nimitz retained Kimmel's entire staff, a calculated move designed to begin rebuilding the Pacific Fleet's shattered confidence.

Within hours of Pearl Harbor, USN Chief of Naval Operations Admiral Harold Stark had ordered carrier *Yorktown*, battleships *New Mexico*, *Mississippi*, and *Idaho*, a destroyer squadron, and three squadrons of patrol bombers to reinforce the Pacific Fleet from the Atlantic. Carrier *Yorktown* departed Norfolk, Virginia for the Pacific on December 16. By now all three Pacific carrier task forces were operating west of Hawaii, although Fletcher and *Saratoga* returned to Pearl Harbor on December 29. The following day, December 30, *Yorktown* reached California. That same day Fletcher was abruptly ordered to catch a flight to San Diego, where he would take command of the new *Yorktown* carrier task force. With Fletcher's departure, Rear Admiral Herbert Leary was elevated to command of *Saratoga*'s TF-14.

On December 24, Pye's staff had stated that the Pacific Fleet's main task was to defend the Hawaii–Midway–Johnston Atoll triangle. They anticipated Japanese carrier raids on outlying positions, and Japanese attempts to capture Samoa and Fiji. Hawaii was to be immediately

Wartime US Pacific Fleet commander Chester W. Nimitz as a rear admiral in May 1941, prior to his appointment to Pacific Fleet command. The soft-spoken Nimitz had already turned downed Pacific Fleet command once, on the belief that he was too junior. (NHHC NH 943)

reinforced, and harassment raids against "a judicious choice of objectives" would attempt to distract the Japanese and hopefully isolate and destroy weak detachments. Surviving US battleship forces would provide "supporting 'strong points' on which ... fast groups could retire."

Indeed, the US Pacific Fleet's battleship force had survived Pearl Harbor relatively intact. Of the Pacific Fleet's nine battleships, only *Arizona* and *Oklahoma* had been irretrievably wrecked, although the severely damaged *West Virginia* and *California* would be out of action until summer 1944. However, *Colorado* had been under refit at Bremerton, on December 7, and thus remained unscathed, while Pearl Harbor's remaining four battleships had received only moderate damage. Escorted by four destroyers, on December 20, 1941 *Pennsylvania*, *Maryland*, and *Tennessee* departed Pearl Harbor for permanent repairs at Bremerton. A fourth Pearl Harbor battleship, *Nevada*, would be refloated on February 12, 1942 before also steaming for major repairs at Bremerton. *Nevada*, however, would only emerge from refit that October.

Additionally, the Atlantic Fleet's modernized battleship *New Mexico* would reach San Francisco on January 22, with her sisters *Idaho* and *Mississippi* joining her a week later, on January 31. *New Mexico* would escort a single California–Hawaii convoy in late January before Nimitz canceled Kimmel's battleships-as-convoy escort mission.

Instead, Nimitz deployed his surviving Pacific Fleet battleships in a temporary defensive role at San Francisco, where they commenced intense training as Task Force 1. By February 1, TF-1 would comprise four fully operational US battleships. *Maryland* and *Tennessee* would additionally return to service on February 26, followed by *Pennsylvania* on March 30. Less than four months after Pearl Harbor the US Pacific Fleet could suddenly boast seven operational battleships ready for action.

REINFORCING THE CENTRAL AND SOUTH PACIFIC

After the Pearl Harbor attack a near-panic reigned amongst the US high command, as Hawaii appeared wide open to invasion. The first US reinforcement convoy of three fast troopships departed San Francisco for Hawaii on December 16, 1941, followed by two more the next day. Incredibly, four days after Pearl Harbor, on December 11, 1941, Japan's nominal allies Nazi Germany and Fascist Italy had suddenly declared war on the United States, allowing the Americans to openly fight the full Axis powers. On December 22, the United States' and Britain's respective chiefs of staff convened as the new Combined Chiefs of Staff to discuss global Anglo-American strategy. The resulting Arcadia Conference reconfirmed "Europe First" as official US strategic policy, with the Anglo-Americans determining an initially defensive strategy in the Pacific, "maintaining only such positions in the Eastern [Pacific] theatre as will safeguard vital interests." However, this also entailed securing "points of vantage from which an offensive against Japan can be eventually developed."

Fortunately, by late December 1941, Hawaii's extreme crisis had abated; it was now apparent from Japan's major offensives in Southeast Asia and the East Indies that Hawaii was not targeted for imminent invasion. Nevertheless, Hawaii was now heavily fortified; by the end of 1941 some 15,000 troops and 77,756 tons of cargo had been shipped to Hawaii since the Pearl Harbor attack.

The primary Allied defensive plan was to hold the so-called "Malay Barrier," best described as an imaginary east–west line extending through Malaya, the Netherlands East Indies, and northern Australia.

Arcadia also established the ultimately forlorn ABDA (American-British-Australian-Dutch) Command in an attempt to unify defense of the Malay Barrier in Southeast Asia and the East Indies.

The initial US reinforcements to Australia had been unplanned. In late November 1941 a US military convoy of seven ships, including crated aircraft and 4,500 troops, had departed Hawaii for Manila, escorted by cruiser *Pensacola*. By December 9 this convoy had been diverted to Brisbane, Australia, arriving safely on December 22. Additionally, Admiral King's ascension to COMINCH on December 31, 1941 brought with it his personal emphasis on holding the lines of communication to Australia.

The sudden strategic emphasis on the South Pacific was wholly unplanned. Nonetheless, in early January 1942 the Combined Chiefs of Staff laid down responsibilities for defending South Pacific territories. The United States would defend Palmyra Island, Christmas Island, Canton Island, Samoa, and Bora Bora in Tahiti, the last currently under Free French administration. Indeed, emphasizing his South Pacific strategy, King directed a major fueling base be established at Bora Bora. However, fewer than 8,000 New Zealand troops and just 22 planes defended the entire Fijis group of 250 islands, while New Caledonia was garrisoned by a single Australian company; both would require American reinforcements.

Only the 2nd and 7th USMC defense battalions had been garrisoning American Samoa when war broke out. On January 6, 1942, Fletcher's TF-17 departed San Diego to escort the convoy to reinforce Samoa. Fletcher's TF-17 comprised carrier *Yorktown*, heavy cruiser *Louisville*, light cruiser *St. Louis*, four destroyers, fleet oiler *Kaskaskia* (AO-27), and the main Samoa convoy of five ships.

On February 14, US Army chief General George C. Marshall would decide to send the US 41st Infantry Division to Australia as reinforcements. The first troops would leave New York in a five-ship convoy on March 3. By mid-March 1942 there would be 34,000 American troops in Australia, with another 23,000 en route.

Nevertheless, as early 1942 dawned, the Allies were forced to defend too much of the Pacific with far too few troops, planes, warships, and merchantmen. The Pacific theater now ironically resembled King's description of his 1941 Atlantic command: "A big slice of bread with damn little butter."

Admiral King poses (quite appropriately) in front of a world map in 1944. King was famously harsh at a time when the post-Pearl Harbor US Navy needed such steel. Even President Roosevelt joked that "King shaves with a blowtorch," while one of King's daughters claimed, "My father is the most even-tempered man in the Navy. He is always in a rage." (NHHC 80-G-K-13715)

CHRONOLOGY

1941

December 7 — Nagumo's six Japanese heavy carriers (Kido Butai) attack and heavily damage the US Pacific Fleet and base at Pearl Harbor.

December 8 — United States declares war on Japan; *Saratoga* departs San Diego for Pearl Harbor.

December 9–10 — IJN Fourth Fleet occupies Makin in northern Gilbert Islands.

December 11 — Germany and Italy declare war on the United States; USMC garrison at Wake Island successfully repulses IJN Fourth Fleet's landing attempt.

December 23 — IJN Fourth Fleet's second landing overruns Wake; US Wake relief attempt aborted.

December 24 — US–Filipino forces evacuate Manila for a final stand on the Bataan Peninsula, effectively signaling Japanese victory in the Philippines.

1942

January 11 — *I-6* torpedoes *Saratoga*, knocking her out of the war for five months.

January 20–23 — Operation *R*: IJN Fourth Fleet forces assault and capture Rabaul and Kavieng.

February 1 — Halsey's and Fletcher's *Enterprise* and *Yorktown* task forces strike the Marshalls and Gilberts.

February 15 — Singapore falls to the Japanese.

February 19 — Nagumo's Kido Butai raids Darwin, Australia.

February 20 — Brown's *Lexington* aborts first attempted US carrier raid on Rabaul after *Lexington* repulses a Japanese bomber attack off Bougainville.

February 24 — Halsey's TF-16 raids Wake with a combined *Enterprise* strike/cruiser bombardment.

March 4 — Halsey's *Enterprise* strikes Marcus Island, less than 1,000 miles from Tokyo.

March 7 — Operation *SR*: IJN Fourth Fleet forces successfully invade Lae and Salamaua in Australian-occupied northeast New Guinea.

March 10 — *Lexington* and *Yorktown* strike occupied Lae and Salamaua by flying their air groups over the Owen Stanley Mountains.

April 18 — Halsey's TF-16 successfully launches USAAF Lieutenant-Colonel James Doolittle's 16 B-25 bombers on a one-way strike against the Japanese Home Islands.

May 4–8 — Fletcher's TF-17 repulses Japanese invasion of Port Moresby at the Battle of the Coral Sea, sinking Japanese light carrier *Shoho*. US carriers *Lexington* sunk and *Yorktown* damaged, IJN carriers *Shokaku* and *Zuikaku* knocked out of the IJN's impending Midway operation.

June 4–6 — Spruance's TF-16 and Fletcher's TF-17 destroy Japanese carriers *Akagi*, *Kaga*, *Soryu*, and *Hiryu* at the Battle of Midway. Carrier *Yorktown* sunk. Midway abruptly ends the Pacific War's first phase, which has been defined by severe Allied military inferiority.

OPPOSING COMMANDERS

JAPANESE

The IJN's Pacific combatant forces were primarily organized into the Combined Fleet, which was largely organized by type. In late 1941 the Combined Fleet's striking forces consisted of the First Air Fleet (carriers), the First Fleet (battle line), the Second Fleet (advance force), the Sixth Fleet (submarines), and the Eleventh Air Fleet (land-based aviation).

Admiral Isoroku Yamamoto was the IJN Combined Fleet commander and Japan's de facto grand strategist in the Pacific. As a former carrier commander, Yamamoto was obsessed with the US carriers his strike had missed at Pearl Harbor, and much of Yamamoto's subsequent Pacific strategy was devoted to countering and hopefully destroying the American carriers.

Yamamoto's primary striking force was the First Air Fleet, commanded by **Vice Admiral Chuichi Nagumo**. These were the six heavy carriers that had attacked Pearl Harbor. Nagumo has been unfairly damned as overly conservative, both by IJNAF contemporaries and by Western historians. Yet between December 1941 and April 1942, Nagumo's Kido Butai conquered all before it in one of the most wildly successful four-month runs in naval history.

In addition to the fleets mentioned above, the Combined Fleet contained several numbered fleets based not on type but on specific geographic locations. The most important of these for the Pacific War was the Fourth Fleet. Also known as the South Seas Force, the Fourth Fleet comprised a fleet of light combatants and assigned air and ground units based in the Central Pacific.[1]

In 1941 the IJN promoted **Vice Admiral Shigeyoshi Inoue** to command Fourth Fleet.

Vice Admiral Shigeyoshi Inoue in a wartime photograph. Inoue was such an outspoken aviation radical that he even rankled his like-minded (but more politically savvy) superior Yamamoto. Inoue was among the last IJN officers promoted to full admiral rank in 1945. He survived the war and died in 1975. (Public Domain)

---

1 For clarity, it should be noted that the existing IJN Fourth Fleet (South Seas Force) would be divided into two separate fleets in summer 1942—the Fourth Fleet (Inner Seas Force) in the north and the brand-new Eighth Fleet (Outer Seas Force) in the south. Under Vice Admiral Gunichi Mikawa, the Eighth Fleet would become infamous for the grievous damage it inflicted on the USN during the Guadalcanal campaign. However, the Eighth Fleet of late 1942 was essentially the old Fourth Fleet.

Rear Admiral Aritomo Goto, Inoue's main Fourth Fleet surface officer, would participate in the IJN's crushing victory at Savo Island on August 8, 1942. Goto would die two months later on October 12, 1942 at the hands of Rear Admiral Norman Scott's force at Cape Esperance, arguably the first USN surface victory of the war. (Public Domain)

Inoue resembled Yamamoto in many respects. Like Yamamoto, Inoue had been a political moderate opposed to the Axis powers and against war with the United States. Although not himself an aviator, Inoue, too, was a strident and uncommonly outspoken naval aviation radical who had openly urged the scrapping of Japanese battleships before the Pacific War. According to Inoue, "He who commands the air commands the sea." Even more than Yamamoto, Inoue grasped the nature of the war Japan was initiating with the United States.

Vice Admiral Eiji Goto commanded the IJNAF 24th Air Flotilla, the land-based naval air force of the Marshall and Gilbert islands. The 24th Air Flotilla's lackluster performance against the US carrier raids ultimately resulted in Goto's transfer to Korea in September 1942. After additional backwater jobs, Goto was put on the inactive list. He resigned from active IJN service in May 1945.

Under Inoue, the 54-year-old **Rear Admiral Aritomo Goto** commanded the IJN's 6th Cruiser Division of four older heavy cruisers, the primary naval striking force organic to Fourth Fleet. A career surface officer experienced in battleships, cruisers, and destroyers, Goto would be killed at the October 12, 1942 Battle of Cape Esperance, becoming the first IJN admiral at sea to die in combat.

Commanding Fourth Fleet's IJN invasion forces was **Rear Admiral Sadamichi Kajioka**. Despite the embarrassing repulse at Wake Island on December 11, 1941, Kajioka remained in command for the second, successful Wake invasion on December 23. Kajioka then led mostly the same Fourth Fleet invasion units in the landings at Lae–Salamaua in March 1942. After commanding the aborted May 1942 Port Moresby invasion force, Kajioka would be killed on September 12, 1944 when submarine USS *Growler* (SS-215) sank destroyer *Shikinami* in the South China Sea.

Captain Susumu Kawasaki (IJN) was Japan's Wake Island garrison commander from January 1942. On December 13, 1942, Kawasaki would be relieved by the infamous IJN Captain Shigematsu Sakaibara, who would massacre all surviving American prisoners at Wake on October 7, 1943.

Commanding the only major IJA component in the Mandates, the so-called South Seas Detachment, was **Major-General Tomitaro Horii**. Horii would drown on November 23, 1942, when his canoe was swept out to sea during the Battle of Buna-Gona.

Rear Admiral Masao Kanazawa would command the IJN 8th Special Base Force when it was established at Rabaul in early 1942.

UNITED STATES

President Franklin Roosevelt promoted 63-year-old **Admiral Ernest J. King** to COMINCH on December 31, 1941. The overbearing and humorless King was famously harsh and demanding; upon his appointment King allegedly observed, "When they get in trouble, they send for the sons-of-bitches." King wisely eschewed an admiral's traditional prerogative of exercising his command at sea, and instead directed the US Fleet from Washington, DC. In March 1942, Roosevelt also named King Chief of Naval Operations (CNO), replacing Admiral Harold Stark. By holding both COMINCH and CNO commands simultaneously, King became the highest-ranking USN officer in history.

King was a strident, even bullying micro-manager. A fully qualified aviator, King had been *Lexington*'s captain between 1930 and 1932. Ironically, despite his strong aviation credentials, King did not grasp the tactical nature of the new Pacific War as well as Nimitz. Personally blunt and undiplomatic, King distrusted subordinate officers with more-than-usual Washington, DC tours, such as Nimitz and Fletcher. King's primary contribution to early Pacific Fleet operations was his vehement insistence on counterattacking the Japanese persistently and immediately.

Admiral Chester W. Nimitz was named Commander-in-Chief Pacific Fleet (CINCPAC) after Pearl Harbor and was therefore King's immediate subordinate. A German-speaking Texan, Nimitz's elegant good looks and relentlessly calm, pleasant demeanor masked a ruthlessly calculating and surprisingly aggressive strategic mind. Despite not being an aviator, Nimitz possessed a shrewd appreciation of the post-Pearl Harbor situation, using his carriers skillfully and understanding that his surviving slow battleships should be husbanded for more favorable opportunities later. Among Nimitz's many subtle talents was an uncanny intuition for sensing which of King's many orders should be carried out and which should be skillfully stonewalled.

Vice Admiral Bill Halsey presided as Commander, Aircraft, Battle Force, a purely administrative command for all Pacific Fleet carriers and air groups. On a tactical level, Halsey personally commanded only the *Enterprise* task force (TF-8/TF-16), although as the Pacific Fleet's senior aviator Halsey also commanded any other carrier forces temporarily assigned to his *Enterprise* group. Unfortunately, Halsey today is largely remembered as an impulsive and reckless buffoon who blundered history's greatest fleet into two deadly typhoons and a near-disaster at Leyte Gulf. But the Halsey of 1941 and early 1942—if recognizable in personality—was a completely different admiral than the caricature of 1944–45. This early-war Halsey has rightly been described as, "More a bull at the gates than a bull in a china shop."

Halsey's *Enterprise* escort screen was commanded by **Rear Admiral Raymond Spruance**, a career surface officer. Although still relatively junior, Spruance's strong performance during the early 1942 raids inspired Halsey

Vice Admiral Bill Halsey in 1941. As a combat commander Halsey was full of uncompromising praise for his men and defiant talk for the Japanese, but—unlike a MacArthur or a Montgomery—always unfailingly modest regarding himself. Indeed, Halsey was a rare populist personality in a USN officer corps that—far more than their Army counterparts—still exuded a pronounced social elitism long out of touch with the rest of America. (NHHC NH 95552)

to wholeheartedly recommend Spruance as TF-16's temporary replacement commander prior to the Battle of Midway. After a stint as Nimitz's chief-of-staff, in late 1943 Spruance was awarded command of the newly established Fifth Fleet, Nimitz's main battle fleet. By August 1945 Spruance would be widely regarded as the USN's greatest ever fleet commander.

Vice Admiral Wilson Brown began the Pacific War as commander TF-11, which was built around carrier *Lexington*. At 60 years old Brown was one of the oldest USN officers to see combat; a prominent Pacific Fleet historian called Brown "an intelligent paragon of old school formality." A nonaviator, Brown had initially been Commander, Scouting Force, but he proved a clever and insightful carrier commander. However, Brown's declining health required his removal from sea command in April 1942 and led to his eventual retirement in late 1944. Consequently, Brown virtually disappeared from the Pacific War and from history.

On December 30, 1941, **Rear Admiral Frank Jack Fletcher** was named commander TF-17, built around carrier *Yorktown*. Fletcher was a decent man and a professional officer—and one of the blandest flag officers ever to inspire such intense historical controversy. Depending on one's biases, Fletcher is perhaps unfairly remembered as a mildly competent admiral at best, or a bumbling coward at worst. That Fletcher would be in overall command at Coral Sea, Midway, and Guadalcanal and never lose a battle has practically been forgotten. Although not conspicuously brilliant or inspiring, Fletcher's main wartime failings were as follows: he had two carrier flagships sunk out from underneath him, he was frequently given conflicting orders in tight spots, and—worst of all—he somehow made abiding enemies out of not just the USN's wartime commander-in-chief Ernest J. King, but the USN's all-authoritative wartime historian, Samuel E. Morison.

King named **Rear Admiral Herbert F. Leary** new ANZAC area commander on January 29, 1942. Leary had commanded TF-14 between December 30, 1941 and *Saratoga*'s torpedoing 12 days later. Leary was a loud, outspoken disciplinarian who apparently made few friends; Nimitz allegedly recommended Leary for ANZAC command partly to remove him from Nimitz's own circle.

An Australian officer serving in the Royal Navy, **Rear Admiral John G. Crace** was commander Australian Squadron. In early 1942 Crace's command fell under Vice Admiral Leary's new American-commanded ANZAC theater and was renamed the ANZAC Squadron. Although Crace naturally craved combat, his American superiors consistently relegated his ANZAC force to the necessary but mundane escort missions well behind the American strike zones.

Future Vice Admiral Wilson Brown photographed while still a rear admiral. Although not an aviator, Brown was a quietly astute carrier officer. The gentlemanly Brown was ultimately relieved due to failing health; his officers nicknamed him "Shaky" for his visible tremors. (Public Domain)

OPPOSING FORCES

JAPANESE

Kido Butai

Yamamoto's primary striking power was Vice Admiral Nagumo's Kido Butai (Mobile Fleet), which was based on the six heavy carriers that had struck Pearl Harbor. These six carriers were divided into three two-carrier divisions. The 1st Carrier Division, or CarDiv-1, comprised the 1920s-era 36,500-ton *Akagi* and 38,200-ton *Kaga*, both converted capital ships. The 2nd Carrier Division (CarDiv-2) consisted of the purpose-built, 1930s-era 15,900-ton *Soryu* and her 17,300-ton half-sister *Hiryu*. Completing Kido Butai was the 5th Carrier Division (CarDiv-5) comprising the superb *Shokaku* and *Zuikaku*. These brand-new sister ships each displaced 26,675 tons and had a top speed of 34 knots. Because of their high speed and large, highly trained air groups, Kido Butai's heavy carriers easily posed the greatest threat to raiding US carriers. Unlike their unblooded US counterparts, the Japanese carriers had seen considerable action off China since 1937. Therefore, in addition to numbers, Kido Butai's primary advantage over US carriers in 1942 was its much greater competence at massing large, coordinated airstrikes.

Japanese Zeroes, Kates, and Vals are readied for launch aboard the Japanese fleet carrier *Zuikaku* in May 1942. The Japanese had major combat and operations experience over the Americans in early 1942, an advantage the US carriers' early Pacific raids did a great deal to close. (Universal History Archive/Getty Images)

IJN Fourth Fleet operations in the South Pacific, December 1941–March 1942

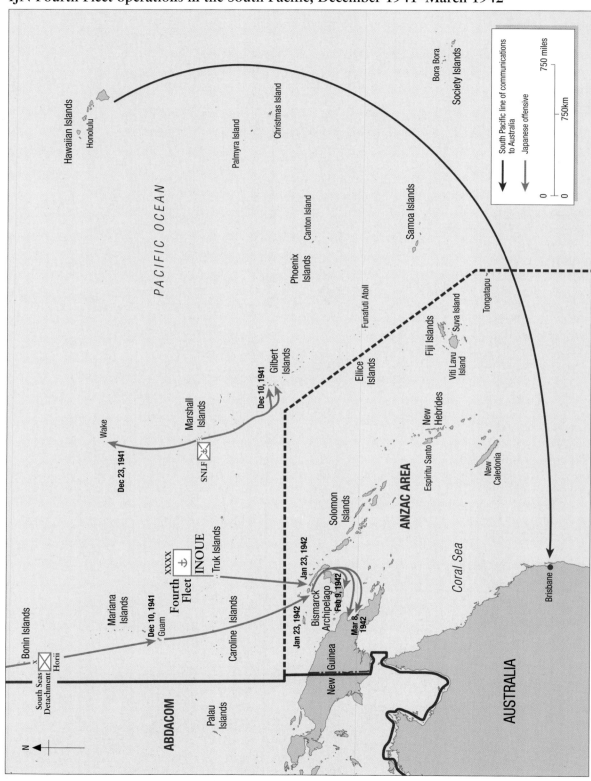

The South Seas Mandate

Inoue's IJN Fourth Fleet, which covered Japan's South Seas Mandate, was headquartered at Truk in the Caroline Islands archipelago. Subordinated to Fourth Fleet was the IJN 6th Base Force, which was headquartered at Kwajalein in the Marshalls. After December 1941 the 6th Base Force controlled the IJN 61st Guard Unit and the IJN 51st, 52nd, 53rd, and 54th Naval Garrison units, which garrisoned the Marshalls, northern Gilberts, and Wake.

The IJN's Special Naval Landing Force (SNLF) units comprised a large naval infantry battalion of about 2,000 men, equipped not just with small arms but also heavy weapons such as howitzers and 3in. naval guns. SNLF troops were expected to embark cruisers and destroyers, which would deliver them ashore and then provide naval gunfire support.

However, the elite, fast-striking SNLF units inevitably became the occupying troops of many of the islands they seized. After early 1942 they slowly transformed into an island defense role and were accordingly redesignated as Base Forces (*konkyochitai*). An IJN Base Force was subordinated to a Fleet and handled administration for ground and surface units. They were also responsible for communications, security, and at times servicing of IJN areas and units. An IJN Special Base Force was deployed near the front lines and assumed tactical responsibilities, for which it was often reinforced. Subordinated to Base Forces and Special Base Force were so-called Naval Guard (or Naval Garrison) units (*keibitai*). These were purely defensive units armed with coastal artillery and antiaircraft batteries. On February 1, the 2nd Maizuru SNLF would be dissolved and re-formed into part of the newly established 8th Special Base Force at Rabaul.

The so-called South Seas Detachment was the IJA's token formation in the Mandates. It comprised a 5,000-man IJA ground unit organized around the 144th Infantry Regiment and was reinforced with its own organic artillery, engineer, reconnaissance, antiaircraft, and logistics units.

Japanese island-based naval and air forces

During the prewar period, virtually every belligerent had automatically assumed that contemporary land-based airpower (particularly high-altitude level bombing by multi-engined bombers) was intrinsically dominant to both surface fleets and carrier-based airpower. The IJN's grand strategy in the Pacific, which was essentially defensive, was built around this purely theoretical concept. However, this maxim proved one of the most incorrect

An *Akagi* A5M Claude seen in 1938 or 1939. The Claude was the direct predecessor to the more famous Zero. In its own day the Claude was as dominant over its adversaries as the later Zero would be. (Public Domain)

peacetime assumptions of World War II, meaning Japan's entire strategy against the United States was therefore based on a flawed premise.

All land-based Japanese naval airpower fell under the IJN 11th Air Fleet, whose 24th Air Flotilla (Dai-Nijuyon Koku-Sentai) was deployed in the South Seas Mandates under the operational control of Inoue's Fourth Fleet.

The primary reconnaissance plane flying from IJN island bases was the Kawanishi H6K4 Mavis flying boat. With its phenomenal endurance, this giant four-engined patrol aircraft was capable of undertaking 24-hour reconnaissance missions. The H6K4 could carry an offensive payload of two 1,764lb torpedoes or 2,205lb of bombs; defensive armament comprised four 7.7mm machine guns and one tail-mounted 20mm cannon.

Fighter protection was provided by the Mitsubishi A5M Claude. Once the world's hottest carrier fighter, the A5M had dominated the skies over China when introduced in early 1937. The Claude was armed with two 7.7mm (0.303) machine guns and was highly maneuverable, with a top speed of 280mph. However, by late 1941 the IJN had relegated the obsolescent Claude to second-line duty at island bases and aboard light carriers.

Introduced in 1936, the Mitsubishi G3M Nell was a land-based, twin-engine bomber that could carry a single torpedo or 1,764lb of bombs on external racks. Its 2,300nm range and 30,000ft ceiling were truly superb; speed was 230mph. The G3M mounted three defensive machine guns, two in a dorsal turret and one in a ventral turret. Although increasingly obsolete, some 204 G3M2 bombers still equipped four Central Pacific air groups (kokutai) in 1942.

The IJNAF's twin-engined Mitsubishi G4M1 Betty bomber (rikujo kogekiki or "land attack plane") boasted a superb combat radius of 600nm while carrying 2,000lb of bombs or a single airdropped torpedo. Top speed was 266mph, with a cruising speed of 195mph. Defensively the Betty was armed with four 7.7mm machine guns, plus a 20mm tail cannon. A complete lack of armor or self-sealing fuel tanks made the Betty ignite easily; the bomber's seven-man crews derisively nicknamed the design the "Type 1 lighter."

The main surface units of Inoue's Fourth Fleet were the 6th Cruiser Division comprising the four older heavy cruisers *Aoba*, *Kako*, *Kinugasa*, and *Furutaka* and the 18th Cruiser Division's two light cruisers *Tenryu* and *Tatsuta*. These operated out of Truk. Various small patrol vessels and auxiliary craft were semi-permanently deployed to the IJN's South Seas Mandate island bases.

UNITED STATES

US Pacific Fleet carrier task forces

In early 1942 US carrier task forces consisted of a single carrier surrounded by an escorting ring of seven to eight cruisers and destroyers, which provided antiair, antisubmarine, and limited antisurface defense. Ideally, each task force was assigned an oiler, which accompanied the task force in safe waters but was temporarily detached during penetrations into enemy waters.

Two carrier task forces were centered around *Lexington* (TF-11) and *Saratoga* (TF-14). *Lexington* and *Saratoga* had originally been laid down as battlecruisers. Because of the Washington Treaty they were converted into 36,000-ton aircraft carriers in 1927. Although fast and elegant, *Lexington* and *Saratoga* were easily the least-maneuverable ships in the US Navy. The remaining two carrier task forces comprised the *Enterprise* (TF-8/TF-16) and *Yorktown* (TF-17) task forces. *Yorktown* and *Enterprise* were 20,100-ton *Yorktown*-class carriers. They had been designed from the keel up as aircraft carriers; despite being smaller than *Lexington* and *Saratoga* they were considerably more efficient.

All carrier operations were dominated by calculations of speed and fuel—hit-and-run raids most of all. Every carrier, cruiser, and destroyer in a US fast carrier task force could theoretically exceed 32 knots. However, such high speeds consumed extreme amounts of fuel oil, meaning maximum speed was typically reserved for imminent combat situations. Additionally, because heavily laden carrier aircraft needed considerable headwind to take off and land on a short deck, carriers always turned into the wind and increased speed as necessary for flight operations. Launching and landing full air groups could require several hours of high-speed steaming, meaning flight operations in low wind forced the task force to burn excessive amounts of fuel. Otherwise, standard task force cruising speed was 20 knots, which was far more economical. Nevertheless, even at 20 knots the extremely short-ranged destroyers needed to be refueled every three to four days.

A task force's oiler would refuel its warships immediately before the high-speed run-in, and then detach to loiter at long range, sometimes escorted by a destroyer. After the raid the oiler would then reunite with its task force and immediately refuel its warships again.

A Brewster F2A-3 Buffalo fighter seen in mid-1942. At this point all surviving US Buffaloes had been relegated to training purposes. In its original configuration the Buffalo had been a fairly nimble fighter, but the final versions were badly weighed down by self-sealing fuel tanks and armor plating they weren't designed for. (Public Domain)

Early Pacific raids and operations, December 1941–March 1942

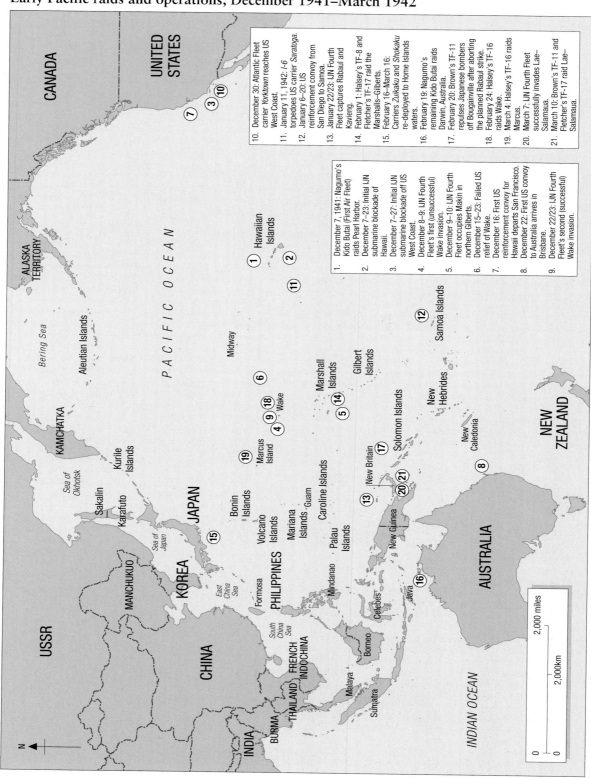

10. December 30: Atlantic Fleet carrier *Yorktown* reaches US West Coast.
11. January 11, 1942: *I-6* torpedoes US carrier *Saratoga*.
12. January 6–20: US reinforcement convoy from San Diego to Samoa.
13. January 22/23: IJN Fourth Fleet captures Rabaul and Kavieng.
14. February 1: Halsey's TF-8 and Fletcher's TF-17 raid the Marshalls–Gilberts.
15. February 16–March 16: Carriers *Zuikaku* and *Shokaku* re-deployed to Home Islands waters.
16. February 19: Nagumo's remaining Kido Butai raids Darwin, Australia.
17. February 20: Brown's TF-11 repulses Japanese bombers off Bougainville after aborting the planned Rabaul strike.
18. February 24: Halsey's TF-16 raids Wake.
19. March 4: Halsey's TF-16 raids Marcus.
20. March 7: IJN Fourth Fleet successfully invades Lae–Salamaua.
21. March 10: Brown's TF-11 and Fletcher's TF-17 raid Lae–Salamaua.

1. December 7, 1941: Nagumo's Kido Butai (First Air Fleet) raids Pearl Harbor.
2. December 7–23: Initial IJN submarine blockade of Hawaii.
3. December 7–27: Initial IJN submarine blockade off US West Coast.
4. December 8–9: IJN Fourth Fleet's first (unsuccessful) Wake invasion.
5. December 9–10: IJN Fourth Fleet occupies Makin in northern Gilberts.
6. December 15–23: Failed US relief of Wake.
7. December 16: First US reinforcement convoy for Hawaii departs San Francisco.
8. December 22: First US convoy to Australia arrives in Brisbane.
9. December 22/23: IJN Fourth Fleet's second (successful) Wake invasion.

24

US carrier air groups

Each US carrier hosted an air group nominally comprising four 18-plane squadrons each operating a different aircraft type: a Fighting squadron (Grumman F4F Wildcat or Brewster F2A-3 Buffalo fighters), a Bombing squadron (Douglas SBD Dauntless scout/dive-bombers), a Scouting squadron (also SBD scout/dive-bombers), and a Torpedo squadron (Douglas TBD Devastator torpedo-bombers). With the carrier air group (CAG) commander flying his own independent plane, a US carrier air group comprised a theoretical 73 aircraft per carrier.

The two-man SBD-3 Dauntless could carry up to 1,600lb of bombs and was armed with two cowl-mounted .50-caliber machine guns and two flexible .30-caliber machine guns mounted in the rear of the cockpit. Top speed was 255mph at 14,000ft. Scouting squadron SBDs were virtually identical to their Bombing squadron counterparts, except to extend their range they lacked self-sealing fuel tanks.

Man for man, in early 1942 the USN's Dauntless crews were likely the best-trained and most formidable practitioners of dive-bombing in the world, exceeding in skill and aggressiveness not just their IJNAF counterparts, but also their more celebrated Luftwaffe rivals flying the notorious Ju 87 Stuka.

By December 1941, *Lexington* was the last US carrier deploying the obsolete Brewster F2A-3 Buffalo fighter; these would be exchanged for F4F-3 Wildcat fighters in February 1942. The single-seat F4F-3 Wildcat fighter had a top speed of 317mph at 16,100ft. The Wildcat was armed with four wing-mounted 0.50-caliber machine guns. Two 100lb bombs could be carried beneath the wings. Wildcat pilots employed creative tactics and teamwork to help counter Japanese fighters' superior maneuverability.

The three-man TBD-1 Devastator could carry a single Mark 13 air-dropped torpedo or 1,000lb of bombs and was armed with a .30-caliber machine gun in the nose and a flexible .30-caliber machine in the rear cockpit. Top speed was just 206mph at 8,000ft.

A US carrier air group's strike coordination was hampered by the disparate performances of its various aircraft types. An SBD armed with a 500lb bomb could strike 225nm from its carrier, or up to 175nm when carrying a 1,000lb

bomb. A TBD's standard strike range when carrying its 2,216lb Mark 13 torpedo was only 150nm but was 175nm when carrying three 500lb bombs for level bombing. The F4F's radius was limited to 175nm, which meant the longest-ranged strikes had to be executed without fighter escort.

US Task Force defense

Extensive 1930s wargames and exercises had convinced the USN that aircraft carriers were virtually impossible to defend from air attack—prewar detection was purely visual, and once enemy bombers were sighted, they were typically already on their attack run (indeed, many early-war air attacks were only detected when bombs began detonating alongside). Prewar carriers were therefore considered severely imbalanced tactically—powerful in scouting and offense, but extraordinarily vulnerable to air attack.

The introduction of radar began to change all this. The USN had begun installing its first precious air-search radar sets, the CXAM-1 model, in US carriers in 1941. The crude CXAM-1 could detect incoming aircraft to a range of 70nm. However, the CXAM-1 could not reliably read altitude, and it presented its return data via the so-called "A scope," which had to be interpreted by a trained radarman and then manually plotted onto a separate chart (the more user-friendly and now-ubiquitous circular chart-style scope, the Plan Position Indicator, was not introduced until late 1942). In addition to the carriers' CXAM-1 sets, some US destroyers mounted the smaller, less-effective SC air-search radar. Radar's ability to detect enemy aircraft well beyond visual range suddenly made carriers potentially survivable from air attack, but it meant radar-guided fighter-direction tactics and equipment had to be developed from scratch.

Consequently, early USN fighter-direction tactics were still primitive and unrefined in both technology and method. Most significantly, in early 1942 the USN had not yet developed the dedicated "Combat Information Center" (CIC). Fighter-direction teams were still shoehorned into a cramped corner of Air Plot within the already crowded and distracting carrier island. Even the iconic vertical plotting board had not yet been adopted by the USN. Because fighter direction was still transmitted MF (Medium Frequency) radio, it could reasonably be intercepted by the enemy. Judicious use of transmissions was required by a fighter director to avoid a position fix by Japanese forces.

The 1.1in. "Chicago Piano" medium antiaircraft gun, seen here in May 1942, was one of the worst weapons of the war. Its four barrels were intended to compensate for its low rate of fire, and it was constantly jamming. It was replaced by the superb 40mm Bofors gun as soon as possible. (Public Domain)

Additionally, IFF (Identification Friend or Foe) equipment and usage was still scarce, meaning a 1942 US fighter director often had to sift through too many "bogies" (unidentified aircraft).

US combat air patrols typically operated within sight of their carrier, in two- to three-hour shifts of four to six fighters, although SBDs were also pressed into this role. Because 1941 US carrier fighters lacked oxygen, 20,000ft was considered the general maximum altitude, and sustained CAPs above even 10,000ft altitude were avoided if possible.

By 1945 USN antiaircraft fire would reign supreme in the world, but in early 1942 the situation was entirely different. The 5in./25 AA gun and 5in./38 Dual-Purpose (DP) gun comprised US warships' long-range antiaircraft artillery. Providing medium antiaircraft fire was the slow and unwieldy 1.1in./75 gun; its quadruple-barreled appearance inspired the nickname "Chicago Piano." In actual operation the mechanically unreliable 1.1in./75 was a chronic jammer, and by 1941 the USN was already searching for a replacement. Light antiaircraft fire was provided by the wholly inadequate Browning M2 .50-caliber machine gun, which fired a 0.1lb projectile at a rate of 500 rounds/min. The Browning's replacement, the superior 20mm Oerlikon, was just coming online.

Potential Atlantic reinforcements

In addition to *Lexington*, *Saratoga*, *Enterprise*, and *Yorktown*, three more US fleet carriers could theoretically reinforce the Pacific Fleet. In December 1941 the brand-new Yorktown-class carrier *Hornet* (CV-8) was still working up in the Atlantic; she was the centerpiece of the new Atlantic-based TF-18, which included cruisers *Vincennes* and *Nashville*, DesDiv-22, and oiler *Cimarron*. King would order TF-18 to depart for the Pacific on February 20, 1942; TF-18 would reach Pearl Harbor in mid-March. *Hornet*, however, had already been designated for the top-secret Doolittle mission; by the time she had completed this assignment in late April, the early 1942 raids were over. The 14,700-ton 1940 carrier *Wasp* (CV-7), a downsized, quasi-*Yorktown*, was temporarily retained in the Atlantic, where she protected North Atlantic convoys and made two "Malta Runs" to deliver RAF Spitfires in the Mediterranean. *Wasp* would not reach the Pacific until June 1942, too late to influence the early carrier raids. Finally, the 14,810-ton 1934 carrier *Ranger* (CV-4) was considered too small, slow, and vulnerable to be risked in the Pacific. *Ranger* would fight two Atlantic actions, but by 1944 would be permanently relegated to training.

Similarly, the ancient pre-World War I battleships *Arkansas*, *New York*, and *Texas* had long been considered too vulnerable against the IJN battle line and would spend all but 1945 in the Atlantic. However, the USN's modern new fast battleships *Washington* and *North Carolina*, commissioned in 1941, outclassed any existing Axis battleships. They would be joined in 1942 by the four modern South Dakota-class battleships. For the time being, however, "Germany First" dictated that the USN's six new fast battleships remain in the Atlantic to counter potential sorties by the modern German fast battleships *Tirpitz*, *Scharnhorst*, and *Gneisenau*. The Pacific Fleet would not welcome its first fast battleship, *North Carolina*, until July 1942.

MARSHALLS–GILBERTS RAIDS ORDERS OF BATTLE, FEBRUARY 1, 1942

JAPANESE

IJN SIXTH FLEET—VICE ADMIRAL MITSUMI SHIMIZU

Kwajalein
Light cruiser *Katori* (Shimizu)
Submarine tender *Yasukuni Maru*
Ammunition ship *Aratama Maru*
Oiler *Toa Maru*
Submarine *I-9*
Submarine *I-15*
Submarine *I-17*
Submarine *I-19*

Submarine *I-23*
Submarine *I-26*
Submarine *RO-61*
Submarine *RO-62*

IJN 6TH BASE FORCE (FOURTH FLEET)—REAR ADMIRAL SUKEYOSHI YATSUSHIRO

Headquarters Kwajalein
6th Base Force Signal Unit
    5 x special signal stations
IJA transport *Bordeaux Maru*
6th Ports and Docks Unit
Freighter *Taito Maru*
Freighter *Yamagiri Maru*
Water tanker *Amakasu Maru No. 1*
Cruiser-minelayer *Tokiwa*
Patrol gunboat *Fukui Maru*
Patrol gunboat *Hakkaisen Maru*
Patrol gunboat *Kaikei Maru*
Patrol gunboat *Kaiun Maru*
Patrol gunboat *Kantori Maru*
Patrol gunboat *Santos Maru*
Patrol gunboat *Toyotsu Maru*

Kwajalein Atoll (Kwajalein and Roi)
IJN 61st Guard Unit (204 troops) (detachment deployed to Kwajalein's Roi island)
Roi Heavy Antiaircraft Battery
Namur Heavy Antiaircraft Battery
Namur Searchlight Detachment
Chitose Kokutai (Roi)—Captain Fujiro Ohashi
    18 x A5M4 Claude fighters—Lieutenant-Commander Shumasa Isoarashi
16th Minesweeper Division (Kwajalein)
    Minesweeper *Showa Maru No. 7*
    Minesweeper *Showa Maru No. 8*
    Minesweeper *Tama Maru No. 3*
    Minesweeper *Tama Maru No. 5*
62nd Subchaser Division (Kwajalein)
    Net-layer *Katsura Maru*
    Patrol craft/subchaser *Takunan Maru No. 6*
    Patrol craft/subchaser *Takunan Maru No. 7*

Wotje Atoll
IJN 53rd Naval Garrison unit (398 troops)
Wotje Radio Receiving Station
Wotje Short Wave Interception Station
Wotje Long Wave Interception Station
Wotje Naval Depot
Wotje Naval Fuel Depot

Maloelap Atoll (Taroa)
IJN 52nd Naval Garrison unit (398 troops)
Maloelap Radio Receiving Station
Maloelap Antiaircraft Battery
Maloelap Heavy Antiaircraft Battery
Chitose Kokutai (detachment deployed to Taroa)—Lieutenant Yoshio Kurakane
    15 x A5M4 Claude fighters (Kurakane)
    9 x G3M2 Nell bombers—Lieutenant Kazuo Nakai
64th Subchaser Division (Taroa)
    Net-layer *Kashima Maru*
    Patrol craft/subchaser *Shonan Maru No. 10*
    Patrol craft/subchaser *Shonan Maru No. 11*

Jaluit Atoll
IJN 51st Naval Garrison unit (398 troops)
Jaluit Heavy Antiaircraft Battery
Yokohama Kokutai (detachment deployed to Jaluit)—Lieutenant-Commander Sanemiro Koizumi
    6 x H6K4 Mavis flying boats
Collier *Shin Yubari Maru*
8th Gunboat Division
    Patrol gunboat *Chokai Maru*
    Patrol monitor *Daido Maru*
    Patrol gunboat *Kiuta Maru*
    Patrol gunboat *Nagata Maru*
63rd Subchaser Division
    Patrol craft *Fumi Maru No. 3*
    Patrol craft *Shonan Maru No. 3*
    Net-layer *Kotobuki Maru No. 3*

Makin Atoll (Gilbert Islands)
IJN 51st Naval Garrison Unit (detachment)
Yokohama Kokutai (detachment deployed to Makin)—Lieutenant Isamu Sakaki
    3 x H6K4 Mavis flying boats

UNITED STATES
MARSHALLS–GILBERTS RAIDS—VICE ADMIRAL WILLIAM F. HALSEY

TASK FORCE 8—VICE ADMIRAL WILLIAM F. HALSEY (*ENTERPRISE*)

Carrier Group—Halsey
CV-6 *Enterprise*—Captain George D. Murray
    Enterprise Air Group—Commander Howard L. Young (1 x SBD-3)
        VF-6—Lieutenant-Commander C. Wade McClusky (18 x F4F-3/3A)
        VB-6—Lieutenant-Commander William R. Hollingsworth (18 x SBD-2/3)
        VS-6—Lieutenant-Commander Hallstead L. Hopping (18 x SBD-2/3)
        VT-6—Lieutenant-Commander Eugene E. Lindsey (18 x TBD-1)
DD-390 *Ralph Talbot*—Commander Ralph Earle, Jr
DD-387 *Blue*—Commander Harold N. Williams
DD-400 *McCall*—Commander Frederick Moosbrugger

Striking Group—Rear Admiral Raymond A. Spruance (*Northampton*)
Wotje Bombardment Group—Spruance
    CA-26 *Northampton*—Captain William D. Chandler
    CA-25 *Salt Lake City*—Captain Ellis M. Zacharias
    DD-384 *Dunlap*—Lieutenant-Commander Virginius R. Roane
Maloelap Bombardment Group—Captain Thomas M. Shock (*Chester*)
    CA-27 *Chester*—Captain Thomas M. Shock

    DD-363 *Balch*—Commander Charles J. Rend
    DD-401 *Maury*—Lieutenant-Commander Elmer D. Snare

Fueling Group
AO-24 *Platte*—Captain Ralph H. Henkle
DD-382 *Craven*—Lieutenant-Commander Allen P. Calvert

TASK FORCE 17—REAR ADMIRAL FRANK "JACK" FLETCHER (*YORKTOWN*)

Carrier Group
CV-5 *Yorktown*—Captain Elliott Buckmaster
    Yorktown Air Group—Commander Curtis S. Smiley (1 x SBD-3)
        VF-42—Lieutenant-Commander Oscar Pederson (18 x F4F-3)
        VB-5—Lieutenant-Commander Robert G. Armstrong (19 x SBD-3)
        VS-5—Lieutenant-Commander William O. Burch, Jr. (19 x SBD-3)
        VT-5—Lieutenant-Commander Joe Taylor (12 x TBD-1)
CA-28 *Louisville*—Captain Elliott B. Nixon
CL-49 *St. Louis*—Captain George A. Rood
DD-410 *Hughes*—Lieutenant-Commander Donald J. Ramsay
DD-409 *Sims*—Lieutenant-Commander Willford M. Hyman
DD-414 *Russell*—Lieutenant-Commander Glenn R. Hartwig
DD-416 *Walke*—Lieutenant-Commander Thomas E. Fraser

Fueling Group
AO-25 *Sabine*—Commander Houston L. Maples
DD-364 *Mahan*—Lieutenant-Commander Rodger W. Simpson

OPPOSING PLANS

JAPANESE

After cynically declaring war on Imperial Germany in August 1914, Japan had quickly captured the German-occupied Mariana, Caroline, and Marshall islands in the Central Pacific (the Marianas' Guam remained an American territory). The 1919 Versailles Treaty ultimately mandated Japan temporary responsibility for these ex-German possessions. Realistically, Versailles legitimized permanent Japanese occupation of these Central Pacific archipelagoes, which became known as the South Seas Mandate or simply "the Mandates." Within a few years the Japanese government was illegally denying access to League of Nations inspectors. In 1933 Japan melodramatically withdrew from the League of Nations, insuring Japan's Central Pacific holdings remained part of its empire.

Japan's basic Pacific War plan was to build a huge perimeter of island bases extending east into the Pacific, and shuttle land-based aircraft, submarines, and light surface forces between these bases as needed to concentrate power against the expected counterattack by the main US fleet. After these perimeter defenses had whittled down the advancing US fleet, the main IJN fleet would engage the Americans and defeat them in a single decisive battle. This battle had originally been expected to take place somewhere east of the Japanese-occupied Mariana Islands. However, the sudden increase in performance of 1930s land-based aircraft caused the IJN to push its Pacific defense perimeter thousands of miles farther east. By late 1936 the IJN began building airfields in Micronesia, particularly the Marshalls. Between 1937 and 1941 the IJN vacillated between heavily defending just the Marianas, or the Marianas and the Marshalls both. Only in late 1941 did the IJN begin fortifying the Marshalls—far too late as it turned out.

The Marshall Islands are 1,800nm north-northwest of Samoa, and lie within a crude rectangle 200nm by 125nm. The Marshalls' Kwajalein is the largest atoll in the world, lying 600nm south of Wake and 900nm northwest of Baker and Howland islands, both minor US possessions. Kwajalein's northern island of Roi possessed a large Japanese airfield. Kwajalein Atoll surrounds a huge lagoon that provided a large, deep anchorage for ships. The atoll's eponymous island, Kwajalein, hosted a seaplane base with H6K flying boats and other seaplanes.

The Marshalls' large and brand-new IJN airbases at Taroa and Roi hosted the Chitose Kokutai of the 24th Air Flotilla, consisting of G3M Nell

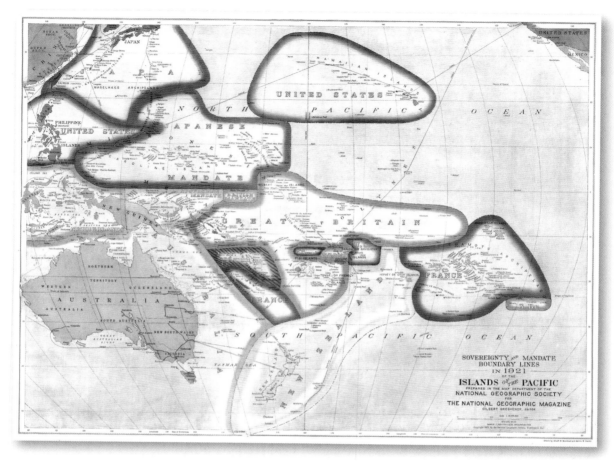

This impressive 1921 map from *National Geographic* magazine illustrates the Pacific's imperial powers, particularly the so-called Mandates awarded by the League of Nations. The United States' pre-existing island domains are in blue, while Japan's Mandates are in magenta in the upper left, and British territories in the center are in bright red. As the League of Nations simply consisted of World War I's victors, the islands' ultimate owners were hardly in doubt. (Public Domain)

bombers and A5M Claude fighters.[2] Unknown to the Americans, Taroa had two well-built crushed-coral runways, with the longest 4,920ft. Taroa also had two hangars and a service apron. US aviators reported that Taroa's airbase compared favorably to Ford Island, the US carriers' main airbase at Pearl Harbor.

Wotje Atoll, in the Marshalls' Ratak chain, comprises 72 islands enclosing a lagoon roughly 24nm east–west and 10nm north–south. At Wotje was an additional Japanese seaplane base.

Jaluit Atoll, in the Marshalls' Ralik chain, is nearly 30nm long and up to 12nm wide, with a total land area of just four square miles. Like Wotje and Kwajalein, Jaluit was also equipped with H6K flying boats and smaller seaplanes.

On December 8, 1941 a company of the IJN 1st Guard Force from Jaluit had landed unopposed on Makin in the British Gilbert Islands and begun building a seaplane base and radio station. This bloodless operation meant the IJN now controlled both the Marshalls and the northern Gilberts. As Japan's outermost outposts in the Central Pacific, the Marshalls and Gilberts would presumably be the Americans' first targets for counterattacks—whether as raids or full-scale offensives. Yet quite illogically, the IJN assigned its Marshalls–Gilberts bases second-rate aircraft instead of the brand-new and modern Zero fighter and Betty bomber.

2 Note: Taroa is *not* Tarawa. Taroa is an island of the Maloelap Atoll in the Marshall Islands, while the now better-remembered Tarawa (the site of the November 1943 US invasion) is its own complete atoll 455nm away in the Gilbert Islands.

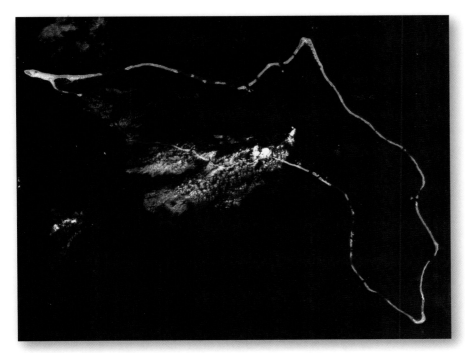

Kwajalein Atoll viewed from an orbiting NASA satellite, February 2003. Kwajalein Island is the southernmost, at the bottom right. The second-largest island, Roi-Namur, is the northernmost island at the top. Kwajalein Atoll boasts the largest lagoon in the world and remains a major US military base. (NASA)

Additionally, in November 1941 Japan's prime minister, the IJA's General Hideki Tojo, had acknowledged that the Home Islands might be hit by a few desultory US carrier raids. Tojo however stressed this was insufficient reason to weaken Japan's upcoming offensive by retaining significant fighter forces in the Home Islands. However, the direct defense of the homeland (and personal protection of the Emperor) against air–sea raids was largely the strategic and moral responsibility of the Pacific-facing IJN, not Tojo's mainland Asia-deployed IJA. Consequently, Yamamoto would prove particularly vulnerable to pulling major carrier units back to the Home Islands.

UNITED STATES

In January 1942, US Pacific Fleet strategy prioritized Samoa reinforcement convoy operations, after which hit-and-run raids would be contemplated. Nevertheless, on January 2, 1942, King messaged Nimitz, "Undertake some aggressive action for effect on general morale." Nimitz coyly responded that such plans "were contemplated and under consideration." King's obsession with immediately counterattacking the Japanese in the face of overwhelming superiority went against all prewar and in-war planning, defied the US high command's "Europe First" consensus, and ignored all subordinate officers' advice, including that of Nimitz. King later explained: "No fighter ever won his fight by covering up—merely fending off the other fellow's blows. The winner hits and keeps on hitting, even though he has to be able to take some stiff blows in order to keep on hitting."

The ever-aggressive King pressed Nimitz to use the Pacific Fleet's surviving battleships alongside the carriers, but Nimitz carefully ignored him. Tactically, the 20-knot battleships were incompatible with the 30-knot speeds required for fast carrier hit-and-runs. During a Japanese aerial attack, the battleships would either have slowed the entire carrier task force, or else been left behind by the fleeing 30-knot carriers, cruisers, and destroyers. Operationally, the US battleships could themselves be run down by any Japanese fleet carrier and most of the Japanese battle line. Finally, as the US battleships could only maneuver at two-thirds the speed of the carriers, they were easier targets for enemy bombers to hit.

Most importantly, in early 1942 Nimitz had only seven oilers available, which his staff calculated could support at most four carriers and their escorts in modest combat operations. Therefore, Nimitz could realistically engage his entire 30-knot carrier force in offensive operations, or a few of his 20-knot battleships—but not both. Under the circumstances in which the USN was forced to operate in early 1942, Nimitz felt the superior choice was obvious.

The Americans' primary advantage was the vast and largely empty Pacific Ocean, as the enormous distances limited the ability of superior Japanese forces to retaliate promptly. Moreover, an alert US carrier task force could outrun heavy Japanese surface forces. The Japanese could and did counterattack with land-based bombers, whose range exceeded that of US carrier aircraft. Additionally, prowling IJN submarines were always a threat. However, because maintaining high speed and the briefest of appearances off Japanese bases was crucial, the greatest threat to raiding US naval forces was simply any lucky bomb or shell hit that crippled an American ship.

Vice Admiral Halsey (front center) with his staff in either late 1941 or early 1942. The Pacific Fleet command structure was in a major state of flux in the year leading up to Pearl Harbor, but by 1942 settled into the Task Force format that survived World War II. Although Halsey himself was not an architect of the Marshalls–Gilberts raids, he was arguably its strongest proponent after King. (NHHC 80-G-464485)

THE CAMPAIGN

COMMANDER MICHIMUNE INABA'S *I-6* TORPEDOES *SARATOGA*, JANUARY 11, 1942

January 6, 1942 found Rear Admiral Herbert Leary's TF-14 headed back to Pearl Harbor from Midway. That same day a *Saratoga* Dauntless on patrol sighted a Japanese submarine cruising on the surface. As the I-boat crash-dived, the Dauntless dropped a 500lb bomb on her, which failed to explode. The next day, presumably the same submarine was spotted 47nm southeast of TF-14. Again the sighting Dauntless attacked, and again the I-boat escaped. By the following day, January 8, the weather had grown so heavy that seas were breaking over *Saratoga*'s bows and flooding her forward elevator, causing flight operations to be suspended for several days.

Meanwhile, *Lexington*'s TF-11 cruised southwest of Hawaii en route to Johnston Island. At 0630hrs, January 9, Commander Kiyonori Otani's *I-18* had sighted *Lexington* and an American cruiser while TF-11 was still 300nm northeast of Johnston Island. Otani duly radioed a sighting report, and IJN Sixth Fleet redeployed several submarines from the Hawaii blockade to the Johnston Island area. However, at 1020hrs, January 10, a *Lexington* scouting patrol sighted the surfaced *I-19* cruising 80nm south of TF-11. A combined attack by two strafing F2A-3 Buffaloes and two depth-charging TBD Devastators forced *I-19* under. *I-19* ultimately escaped to safely return to Kwajalein.

Fast carrier *Saratoga* viewed in an original color photograph in 1942—most likely in June, following *Saratoga*'s return to the fleet following torpedo damage. Built on a former battlecruiser hull, *Saratoga* just missed the Battle of Midway by two days. (NHHC 80-G-K-459)

Vice Admiral Herbert Fairfax Leary was a forceful and outspoken US commander. Unsurprisingly, he came into conflict with US Army General Douglas MacArthur, and in September 1942 he was sent home. After briefly commanding US battleships, Leary would command the Eastern Sea Frontier on the US East Coast from 1943 through the end of the war. Public Domain)

Saratoga was still fighting through exceedingly heavy seas on January 11, yet again forcing flight operations to be suspended. However, *Saratoga* was now being stalked by Commander Michimune Inaba's *I-6*. That evening, while *Saratoga* was 420nm southwest of Pearl Harbor, Inaba maneuvered to within 4,700 yards of *Saratoga* and fired a salvo of three torpedoes. A 1915hrs *Saratoga* was struck in her port beam by a single Japanese torpedo, rocking the carrier with a "terrific explosion" that penetrated three firerooms. Although heavily damaged, *Saratoga* could still make 16 knots, although she had suffered six men killed. Leary was forced to head for Pearl Harbor. Meanwhile, Inaba signaled that he had "sunk" a *Lexington*-class carrier; a Japanese newspaper later reported, "It may well be that this exploit is equivalent to sinking three [battleships] of the enemy."

However, *Saratoga* was still able to conduct flight operations, and she dispatched an SBD scouting patrol the following morning, January 12. One of them sighted an I-boat and attacked it with a 500lb bomb, with inconclusive results. Shortly after midday *Saratoga* briefly lost headway when water contaminated her fuel oil line, but power was ultimately restored. *Saratoga* safely made it back into Pearl Harbor on January 13. She was joined in port by *Lexington* on January 16, and the following day Nimitz reluctantly decided to send *Saratoga* back to the US West Coast for major repairs.

With *Saratoga* out of action, Nimitz accordingly dissolved TF-14 and redistributed its elements to active task forces. After intermediate repairs at Pearl Harbor, *Saratoga* would finally depart Hawaii for Bremerton on February 9. Escorted by four destroyers and embarking ten of her own VF-2 Wildcat fighters purely for defense, *Saratoga* was technically flagship of the ostensible TF-19. The task force safely reached Puget Sound on February 16. *Saratoga*, the first US carrier ever damaged in action, would be *hors de combat* for the next five months.

Otherwise, IJN submarine activity remained persistently harassing but curiously underachieving. The same day *Saratoga* was torpedoed, January 11, Commander Takashi Yamada's *I-20* had surfaced before sunrise and fired a handful of 5.5in. shells into the Tutuila naval station at American Samoa. Damage was inconsequential but the raid reinforced Pacific Fleet anxieties about a Japanese move against Samoa. Additionally, Japanese submarines often shelled Midway Island while coming and going into the Central and Eastern Pacific. The Americans extracted some payback on January 27, when submarine USS *Gudgeon* (SS-211) discovered *I-73* some 200nm west of Midway and sank her, the first US submarine kill of the war.

US PACIFIC FLEET CARRIER PLANS, JANUARY 1942

Back on December 14, Admiral Harold Stark had directed that a fast convoy out of San Diego transport the 2nd Marine Brigade (4,800 men) to Samoa as reinforcements. The Samoa convoy was made up of the ammunition ship

Lassen (AE-3), oiler *Kaskaskia*, freighter *Jupiter* (AK-43), and the three Matson liners *Matsonia*, *Monterey*, and *Lurline*. This convoy would depart from San Diego on January 6, bound for Tutuila, Samoa. It would be directly escorted the entire way by Fletcher's TF-17, based around carrier *Yorktown*. Simultaneously, Nimitz's planners urged a US carrier raid on the Marshalls and Gilberts, planning on Brown's *Lexington* to hit the Marshalls on January 14 and *Enterprise* to strike the Gilberts on January 17; these raids would provide a diversion away from the inbound marine convoy, scheduled to arrive at Samoa on January 20.

After a fruitless Central Pacific patrol, *Enterprise* arrived back in Pearl Harbor on January 7, carrying Vice Admiral Bill Halsey. Halsey was immediately enthusiastic about the proposed Marshalls–Gilberts plan and helped overcome substantial resistance to it. The plan was heavily evolved, largely to undertake the Samoa mission and Marshalls–Gilberts strikes sequentially instead of simultaneously, and on January 9 it was ultimately adopted in substantially modified form. This would allow *Enterprise* and *Yorktown* to protect the Samoa reinforcements before undertaking the USN's first offensive action of the war. Nevertheless, one immediately recognizes Kimmel's old "Marshalls Reconnaissance and Raiding Plan" that had been partially attempted during the December 1941 Wake fiasco.

On January 11, Halsey's TF-8 departed Hawaii to rendezvous with TF-17 and the inbound Samoa convoy. After this mission was completed, Halsey was to assume command of both TF-8 and TF-17 and strike either the Marshalls or Gilberts, with targets left to Halsey's discretion. Nimitz's brief written orders insisted the strike's purpose was to cause damage and collect intelligence on the islands, although "the actual objective was to satisfy King and to improve American morale." In fact, there was no available intelligence on what kind of enemy forces or installations might exist in either island group, because the Japanese had forbidden foreign visits to the Marshalls during their 20 years of occupation.

Nimitz had planned on deploying two carriers in the Central Pacific and two in the South Pacific, but after *Saratoga*'s February 11 torpedoing Nimitz's carrier strength had been reduced 25 percent at a stroke. That left only *Lexington* available to defend the Central Pacific. On January 19, *Lexington* duly sortied from Pearl Harbor to cruise off Christmas Island, some 1,100nm south of Oahu. *Lexington* would function as a distant reserve for the planned *Enterprise–Yorktown* raid against the Marshalls and Gilberts.

OPERATION *R*: THE JAPANESE INVASION OF RABAUL AND KAVIENG, JANUARY 20–23, 1942

Australia's Territory of New Guinea had been captured from Germany in 1914. New Guinea's administrative capital was the port of Rabaul, population 4,000 and virtually the only significant town on the island of New Britain. Accompanying Rabaul on the nearby island of New Ireland was the territorial capital Kavieng, population 4,000. By January 1942 New Britain's garrison had grown into the 1,400-strong "Lark Force" whose cadre was a single battalion, the II./22nd Australian Infantry Force. Rabaul had two nearby airfields, Vunakanau and Lakunai, while Rabaul's excellent Simpson Harbour hosted a seaplane base. The harbor's approaches were

The Rabaul invasion fleet marshals at Truk for Operation *R*. It was photographed on January 9, 1942 by an RAAF Lockheed Hudson on an extremely long-range photoreconnaissance flight. The invasion would take place in two weeks and was the most southeasterly expansion planned by Japan before the war. (Public Domain)

covered by two old 6in. coast defense guns. Rabaul's total air and antiair assets were two 3in. antiaircraft guns, seven obsolete CAC Wirraway planes, and a few Lockheed Hudsons.

Vice Admiral Inoue understood that if the Allies based heavy bombers at Rabaul, they would be in range of his Fourth Fleet headquarters and main base at Truk. Inoue successfully convinced Combined Fleet to make the Rabaul–Kavieng area a target to be invaded in the "First Operational Phase." Dubbed Operation *R*, the combined invasion of Rabaul and Kavieng would be the furthest southeast the IJN had planned to advance in its "First Operational Phase." As it fell within Fourth Fleet's operational area, Inoue was awarded overall command. For air support, Yamamoto temporarily loaned Inoue Nagumo's Kido Butai carrier force, ensuring the invasions' success.

On January 17, carriers *Akagi*, *Kaga*, *Shokaku*, and *Zuikaku*, battleships *Hiei* and *Kirishima*, heavy cruisers *Tone* and *Chikuma*, light cruiser *Abukuma*, and nine destroyers sortied from Truk. Three days later, on January 20, Nagumo's four carriers hit Rabaul with over 100 aircraft, destroying Rabaul's defending planes and coastal artillery. Under carrier air cover, over 3,000 Japanese troops landed at New Ireland early on January 22 and quickly occupied the abandoned town of Kavieng, then captured Kavieng's airfield after brief but fierce Australian resistance.

Major-General Horii's South Seas Detachment landed in New Britain in the early dark of January 23. Within 24 hours Horii's 5,000 troops had scattered the II./22nd Battalion and captured the town of Rabaul and nearby Lakunai airfield. The Japanese had lost 16 dead and 15 wounded, while the Australians had lost 28 men.

Their mission complete, *Akagi* and *Kaga* retired for Truk on January 23, eventually followed by *Shokaku* and *Zuikaku*. *Akagi* and *Kaga* reached Truk on January 25 followed by *Shokaku* and *Zuikaku* two days later. *Shokaku* was shortly detached to Yokosuka. According to *Akagi*'s Commander Mitsuo Fuchida: "All in all, [our] employment … in this operation struck me as extravagant. If ever a sledgehammer had been used to crack an egg, this was the time."

BROWN'S ABORTED TASK FORCE 11 RAID AGAINST WAKE, JANUARY 23, 1942

Vice Admiral Wilson Brown's TF-11 had sortied from Pearl Harbor on January 19, with *Lexington*, three heavy cruisers, and nine destroyers. Brown's destination was northeast of Christmas Island, where he would patrol and await the developments of the planned Marshalls–Gilberts raids by *Enterprise* and *Yorktown*.

By now US intelligence had begun detecting the transfer of Japanese forces to the South Pacific for what would prove to be the January 20–23 invasion of Rabaul and Kavieng. Japan's Central Pacific defenses now appeared

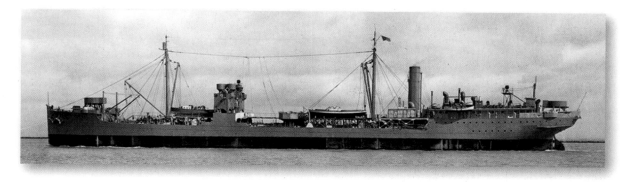

Fleet oiler USS *Neches* (AO-5), viewed sometime before war broke out. *Neches'* top speed of 13 knots greatly limited her utility. *Neches'* assignment to Fletcher's ill-starred 1941 Wake relief task force was one of the many reasons the mission failed. (NARA)

vulnerable to US carrier attack. On January 20 King suggested to Nimitz that Halsey's and Fletcher's raids be expedited, and that an additional force hit Wake. The following day, January 21, Nimitz ordered Brown's TF-11 to raid Wake with a *Lexington* air strike.

Brown would have to refuel during his Wake approach. However, Brown had no oiler with him in TF-11, so at 1700hrs, January 22, Nimitz dispatched his one oiler available at Pearl Harbor, the ancient *Neches* (AO-5), to intercept and refuel the Wake-bound TF-11 on January 27. However, destroyers were so scarce that Nimitz had been forced to send the 13-knot *Neches* out from Pearl Harbor unaccompanied. To provide *Neches* with escort, Brown had detached destroyer *Jarvis* (DD-393) to race ahead and rendezvous with *Neches* the morning of January 23.

However, at 0300hrs, January 23, Japanese submarine *I-72* discovered the unescorted *Neches* 135nm southwest of Pearl Harbor. *I-72* slammed three torpedoes into *Neches* before surfacing and opening fire with her 4.7in. deck gun. The dying *Neches* retaliated with her own portside 5in. and 3in. guns, driving *I-72* under, before sinking at 0400hrs with 57 dead. The arriving *Jarvis* would rescue most of *Neches'* 126 survivors by noon, although *Neches'* skipper would only be picked up several days later in his pajamas. With *Neches* sunk, Nimitz was forced to recall Brown's Wake strike. Late on January 23, TF-11 turned about and headed back to Pearl Harbor while *I-72* escaped back to Kwajalein.

HALSEY AND FLETCHER RAID THE MARSHALLS AND GILBERTS, FEBRUARY 1, 1942

Fletcher's TF-17/USMC convoy reached Samoa on January 20. By January 23 the USMC convoy had fully unloaded at Samoa, protected by the *Enterprise* and *Yorktown* task forces. Two days later TF-8 and TF-17 departed Samoa, heading northwest towards the Marshalls–Gilberts. On January 28 the task forces were refueled underway while northeast of Howland Island. Oiler *Platte* (AO-24) and destroyer *Craven* (DD-382) then retired for Pearl Harbor, but oiler *Sabine* (AO-25) and destroyer *Mahan* (DD-364) were to steam eastward to make a refueling rendezvous with the returning strike forces on February 2.

After a January 27 reconnaissance report by submarine USS *Dolphin* (SS-169) indicated that the Marshalls were less heavily defended than previously thought, Halsey expanded his strike plan, later observing, "It was one of those plans which are called brilliant if they succeed and foolhardy if they

Raid on the Marshall and Gilbert Islands, February 1, 1942

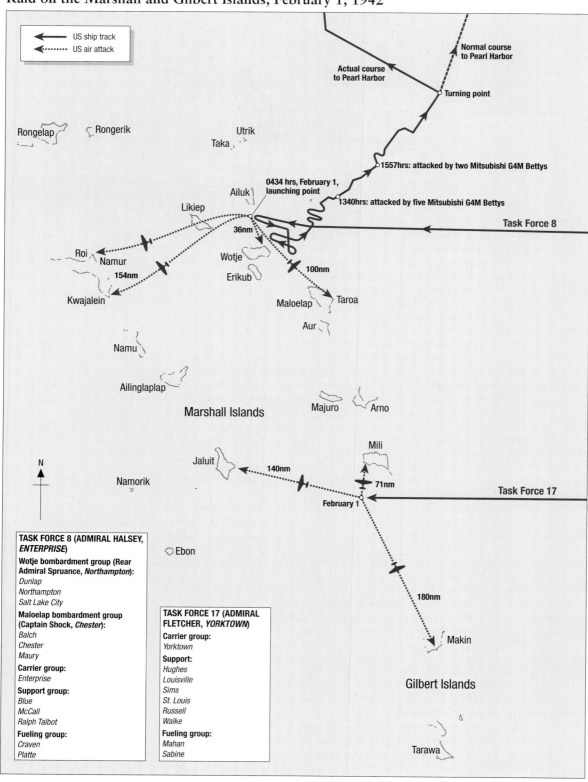

Legend:
→ US ship track
◄····· US air attack

Normal course to Pearl Harbor

Actual course to Pearl Harbor

Turning point

Rongelap Rongerik Utrik Taka

1557hrs: attacked by two Mitsubishi G4M Bettys

0434 hrs, February 1, launching point

Ailuk

1340hrs: attacked by five Mitsubishi G4M Bettys

Likiep

36nm

Task Force 8

Roi Namur Wotje Erikub

100nm

154nm

Taroa

Kwajalein Maloelap

Aur

Namu

Ailinglaplap

Marshall Islands Majuro Arno

Mili

Jaluit 140nm 71nm

Namorik February 1 Task Force 17

N

Ebon

TASK FORCE 8 (ADMIRAL HALSEY, *ENTERPRISE*)

Wotje bombardment group (Rear Admiral Spruance, *Northampton*):
Dunlap
Northampton
Salt Lake City

Maloelap bombardment group (Captain Shock, *Chester*):
Balch
Chester
Maury

Carrier group:
Enterprise

Support group:
Blue
McCall
Ralph Talbot

Fueling group:
Craven
Platte

TASK FORCE 17 (ADMIRAL FLETCHER, *YORKTOWN*)

Carrier group:
Yorktown

Support:
Hughes
Louisville
Sims
St. Louis
Russell
Walke

Fueling group:
Mahan
Sabine

180nm

Makin

Gilbert Islands

Tarawa

A Kawanishi H6K Mavis floatplane, date and location unknown. The Mavis was able to patrol at extremely long ranges and attack anything it found with either bombs or torpedoes. Although not particularly glamorous, the Mavis performed its mission as well as any aircraft in World War II. (Public Domain)

fail." Halsey's TF-8 and Fletcher's TF-17 would strike simultaneously at dawn, February 1. Halsey's *Enterprise* would strike Kwajalein, Roi, Wotje, and Taroa in the northern Marshalls, while two surface detachments would separately shell the Marshalls islands of Wotje and Maloelap. Farther south, Fletcher's *Yorktown* would strike Mili and Jaluit in the southern Marshalls, plus Makin in the northern Gilberts. Unlike Halsey, Fletcher would choose not to detach any escorts for surface bombardments.

For two months US forces had suffered an unbroken string of maulings from Hawaii to Wake to Luzon. Now, for the first time, US forces were venturing into the lion's den. The unblooded Americans were predictably tense. On the afternoon of January 31, *Enterprise*'s air-search radar detected an approaching Japanese patrol plane. As Halsey described it:

We crouched over the screen, watching him close our formation and waiting for his radio to broadcast the alarm. Although he came within 34 miles, the haze evidently hid us, because he serenely continued his patrol. When he disappeared, I sent for my Japanese language officer and gave him a message:

From the American admiral in charge of the striking force, to the Japanese admiral on the Marshall islands ... It is a pleasure to thank you for having your patrol plane not sight my force.

This was translated into Japanese, and our planes dropped copies the next morning, in the hope that the pilot would be shot or have to commit hara-kiri.

At 1830 on the thirty-first, the task groups split up for the run-in to their different stations. The night was clear and calm, and I was the exact opposite. As a commanding officer on the eve of his first action, I felt that I should set an example of composure, but I was so nervous that I took myself to my emergency cabin, out of sight. I couldn't sleep. I tossed and twisted, drank coffee, read mystery stories, and smoked cigarettes. Finally I gave up and went back to flag plot. There, at about 0300, less than 2 hours before we were due to launch, I received a terrifying report. The staff duty officer, Lt. Comdr. S. Everett Burroughs, Jr., came in from the bridge and announced, "Sir, sand has just blown in my face!"

I have already said that the Marshalls area had long been *kapu* (taboo, forbidden, keep out). We knew that our charts were old and we were afraid that they were incomplete and inaccurate as well. (Of course, even the best navigation charts don't show minefields.) When sand blows onto a ship, there is a strong suggestion that land is close aboard; and when the ship is making 25 knots, there is a further suggestion that the situation will clarify quickly and violently.

I could do nothing but tell Evvie to go out and investigate. He returned in a moment, grinning. Suddenly inspired, he had licked his fingers, pressed them against the sand on the deck, and licked them again. The "sand" tasted sweet. On the range-finder platform forward of the bridge, he could dimly make out a sailor stirring a cup.

In fact, neither US carrier force had been sighted, but overnight Fletcher's TF-17 had unknowingly passed within 200nm of the Japanese auxiliary cruisers *Hokoku Maru* and *Aikoku Maru*, returning from a commerce raiding expedition in the Southeast Pacific.

Halsey's attack on Kwajalein, February 1

US intelligence was indeed correct that Japan's Rabaul offensive had stripped the Central Pacific of Japanese bomber strength. Out of a nominal 35 G3M Nell medium bombers and 27 H6K Mavis flying boats assigned to the Marshalls and Gilberts, just nine G3Ms and nine H6Ks remained. In addition to the 18 Japanese bombers were 33 A5M Claude fighters. With 73 operational aircraft aboard *Enterprise* and 60 aboard *Yorktown*, Halsey had a combined 133 planes to face 51 Japanese aircraft.

As darkness fell on January 31, *Enterprise* and her cruisers separated, *Enterprise* increasing speed to 30 knots and the cruisers to 25 knots. Striking Kwajalein would require Halsey to bring *Enterprise* almost on top of Wotje. "To bring a carrier within visual distance of an enemy-held position is not considered good practice," Halsey observed wryly.

At 0443hrs, February 1, *Enterprise* began launching the first of 37 SBDs, each armed with one 500lb bomb and two 100lb bombs. Launching behind the SBDs were nine TBDs armed with three 500lb bombs each. Following the bombers aloft at 0610hrs were 12 Wildcat fighters. Armed with 100lb bombs, six Wildcats each were to smother the airfields at Wotje and Taroa at Maloelap Atoll. However, one F4F and its pilot were lost on takeoff. *Enterprise*'s remaining six fighters would stay behind to fly CAP over the task force.

Led by CAG skipper Commander Howard L. Young, the initial 46 bombers formed up over *Enterprise* and at 0630hrs departed towards Kwajalein Atoll 154nm to the west-southwest. The SBDs' target was the airfield at Roi, while the TBDs would conduct high-altitude level bombing of Kwajalein's lagoon anchorage and seaplane base.

February 1, 1942: an *Enterprise* crewman carries belts of ammunition to load in aircraft bound for the Marshalls. Commanded by the aggressive Halsey, *Enterprise*'s vigorous air action contrasts favorably with the single strike launched by Fletcher's *Yorktown* to the south. (NH 50941)

As the *Enterprise* strike neared Kwajalein, the SBDs sighted land at 0653hrs. However, horizon-level mist prevented them from identifying it as Roi for several minutes. The delay allowed Roi to scramble its fighters, and at least ten A5M Claudes were in the air or getting airborne by 0705hrs, when the SBDs began a shallow glide-bomb attack on Roi's airfield with their 100lb bombs.

In the ensuing aerial melee, three of the unescorted SBDs fell to Claudes or antiaircraft fire, including the attack leader Lieutenant-Commander Hallsted L. Hopping. The SBDs returned fire from their rear-cockpit positions, prompting a bizarre display of airshow-type acrobatic stunts from the Claudes. "They looped together," recalled an SBD pilot, "and followed with an elegant slow roll ... I can't guess what was in their minds." Despite the inexplicable maneuvers, one Claude fell to an SBD gunner before the surviving SBDs escaped into scattered clouds.

Meanwhile, Lieutenant-Commander Eugene E. Lindsey's nine bomb-carrying TBDs of VT-6 arrived over Kwajalein Atoll's main island of Kwajalein and encountered unexpectedly heavy and accurate Japanese flak, but no fighters. At 0658hrs the TBDs began attacking several Japanese freighters in the lagoon, plus two parked H6K Mavis bombers and a compound.

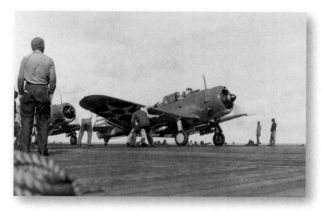

An SBD Dauntless of either VB-6 or VS-6 prepares to launch from *Enterprise* for a target in the Marshalls on February 1, 1942. To preserve their range, the Scouting squadron SBDs had not been equipped with cockpit armor and self-sealing fuel tanks like their Bombing squadron counterparts had. (NNAM.1996.253.599)

Lindsey's TBDs departed Kwajalein at 0717hrs and would be back aboard *Enterprise* by 0935hrs. But before they left, one of Lindsey's TBDs radioed that "two carriers" were present in the Kwajalein lagoon. Commander Young immediately ordered ten of his SBDs to break off the Roi attack and reinforce Lindsey's TBD strike against the Kwajalein anchorage some 40nm away. However, when they arrived at 0725hrs, Young observed only light cruiser *Katori*, ancient cruiser-minelayer *Tokiwa*, four large freighters or tankers, and the seven I-boats.

Young's just-arrived SBDs promptly dove on the Kwajalein flotilla, which retaliated with antiaircraft fire. Three SBDs claimed hits on light cruiser *Katori*, the Sixth Fleet flagship. The blasts wounded Sixth Fleet's commander, Vice Admiral Mitsumi Shimizu. Submarine tender *Yasukuni Maru* was moored in between submarines *I-23* and *I-26*. The submarine crews were loading stores aboard when they came under attack. As the submarines retaliated with antiaircraft fire, one 500lb bomb hit *Yasukuni Maru* on her after 6in. turret, spraying the submarines with shrapnel. American strafing added to the chaos. However, Kwajalein's lagoon is over 150ft deep, and all seven I-boats, including the damaged *I-23* and *I-26*, would eventually submerge to avoid further damage.

The Americans damaged several additional freighters. However, the SBDs' bombs had been fused for instantaneous detonation on ground targets, rather than the delayed fuses preferable for penetrating ships' decks. Despite

Japanese light cruiser *Katori*, a training cruiser, seen sometime in 1940. At the time of the Marshalls–Gilberts raids in February 1942, *Katori* had been assigned to the South Seas Mandates as a flagship for the forward-deployed, submarine-based Sixth Fleet. (Public Domain)

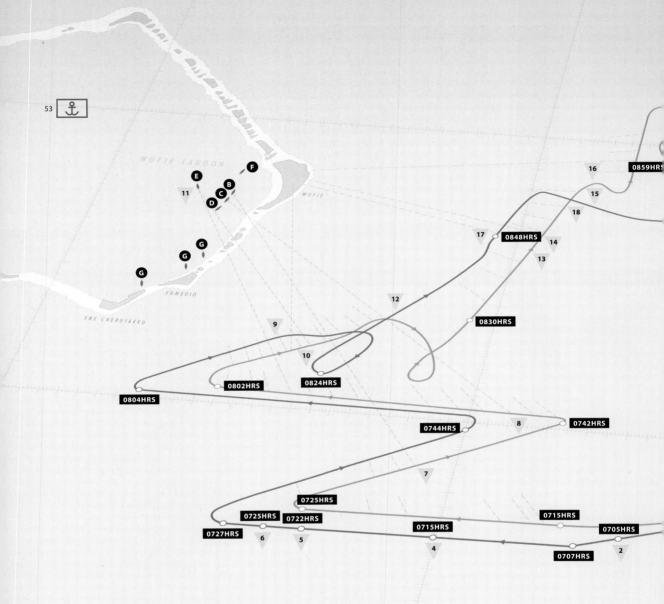

▼ EVENTS

1. *Northampton* launches four floatplanes between 0622hrs and 0639hrs.

2. 0705hrs: *Northampton* and *Salt Lake City* increase speed to 20 knots.

3. 0709hrs: Destroyer *Dunlap* engages Japanese auxiliary gunboat *Toyotso Maru* outside lagoon and sinks her at 0736hrs.

4. 0715hrs: Bombardment commences. *Northampton* opens 8-inch battery fire on merchantman in Wotje lagoon at 24,000yds range.

5. 0722hrs: *Northampton* salvo straddles Japanese merchantman in lagoon.

6. 0725hrs: Japanese merchantman returns fire on *Northampton* with medium-caliber guns.

7. 0733hrs: *Salt Lake City* opens 8-inch battery fire on her first naval target in Wotje lagoon. Range is 20,650yds.

8. 0746hrs: *Salt Lake City* opens 8-inch battery fire on second naval target at range 19,000yds. This second vessel is later observed listing heavily.

9. 0809hrs: Japanese shore battery observed opening fire on *Northampton*.

10. 0811hrs: First big fire observed on Wotje; shore battery silenced.

11. 0812hrs: *Salt Lake City's* third naval target in Wotje lagoon, auxiliary net-layer *Kashima Maru*, is sunk by 8-inch shells.

12. 0816hrs: Submarine periscope reported to portside of US formation, inspiring evasive maneuvers on behalf of US ships. The report is probably false.

13. 0838hrs: *Salt Lake City* observes second large fire in palm trees on Wotje.

14. 0839hrs: *Salt Lake City* targets Japanese shore battery.

15. 0842hrs: *Salt Lake City's* 5-inch battery salvo scores against Japanese hangars ashore.

16. 0843hrs: Japanese shore battery salvo falls near *Salt Lake City*.

17. 0848hrs: Salvo from Japanese shore battery falls 100yds short of *Northampton*.

18. 0855hrs: US warships fire last salvos of Wotje bombardment.

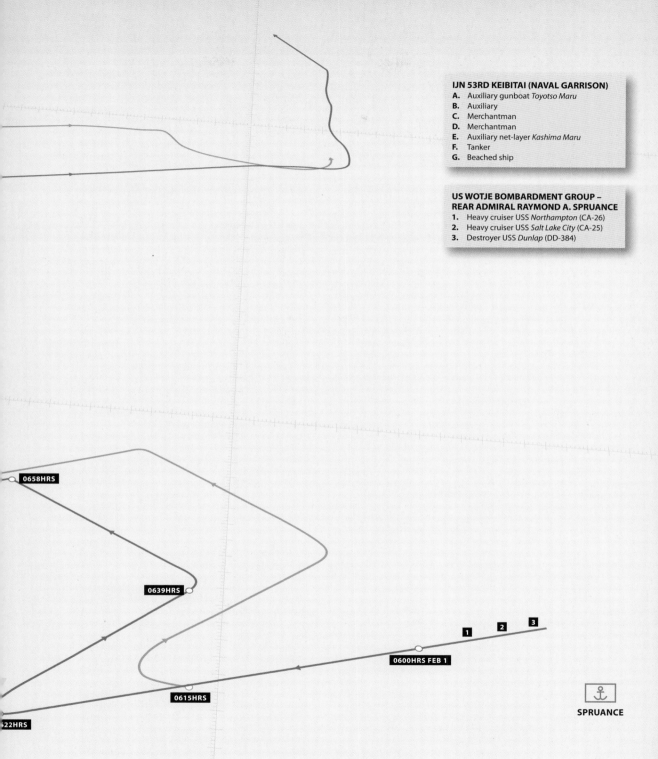

IJN 53RD KEIBITAI (NAVAL GARRISON)
A. Auxiliary gunboat *Toyotso Maru*
B. Auxiliary
C. Merchantman
D. Merchantman
E. Auxiliary net-layer *Kashima Maru*
F. Tanker
G. Beached ship

**US WOTJE BOMBARDMENT GROUP –
REAR ADMIRAL RAYMOND A. SPRUANCE**
1. Heavy cruiser USS *Northampton* (CA-26)
2. Heavy cruiser USS *Salt Lake City* (CA-25)
3. Destroyer USS *Dunlap* (DD-384)

0658HRS

0639HRS

1   2   3

0600HRS FEB 1

0615HRS

22HRS

SPRUANCE

the impromptu weapons, the Americans sank IJA transport *Bordeaux Maru*, killing three Japanese.

By now, VT-6 skipper Lieutenant-Commander Eugene Lindsey had already radioed back to *Enterprise* that the situation in the lagoon was ideal for a torpedo strike. Responding to Lindsey's suggestion, at 0731hrs *Enterprise* launched her last nine TBDs against Kwajalein, armed with torpedoes. By the time Lieutenant-Commander Lance Massey's ponderous TBDs had reached the Kwajalein anchorage at 0905hrs, the earlier SBD strike had already departed and pillars of smoke rose from previously damaged ships.

Recognizing the visibly crippled *Katori* fleeing the lagoon, Massey called out, "Get that cruiser that's headed off to the right! Take them home boys, take them home!" With *Katori* erupting antiaircraft fire, the TBDs put two of their decrepit Mark 13 torpedoes into the water. One detonated prematurely before reaching *Katori*, although the second may have scored against the cruiser.

Massey's remaining TBDs continued across the lagoon, just off the water, and dropped their remaining torpedoes at the submarine tender *Yasukuni Maru* and oiler *Toa Maru*; whether any of these torpedoes scored remains unclear. *Katori* was observed to be dead in the water and down by the bow. Three additional ships were seen to be listing and surrounded by massive oil slicks, and *Yasukuni Maru* was down by the stern and attempting to beach herself. Attempting to shoot down the TBDs the Japanese ships were seen to be firing antiaircraft rounds into each other, while coastal batteries also fired into the ships. All nine TBDs safely returned to *Enterprise* by 1130hrs.

Halsey's attack against *Wotje*, February 1

Rear Admiral Spruance would shell Wotje with heavy cruisers *Northampton*, *Salt Lake City*, and destroyer *Dunlap* (DD-384), while a second detachment of heavy cruiser *Chester* (CA-27) and destroyers *Balch* (DD-363) and *Maury* (DD-401) bombarded Maloelap. Ships in the lagoon were first-priority targets, followed by fixed installations.

Around 0620hrs, February 1, Spruance's Wotje bombardment group began catapulting their spotter planes. Moments later an 800-ton Japanese patrol boat fired a rocket to warn the Wotje garrison, then began closing on the US task group. "Take it," Spruance ordered to *Dunlap*. The Japanese patrol boat made evasive maneuvers, and *Dunlap* could only bring her forward gun to bear, giving her considerable difficulty in hitting the enemy.

With *Enterprise* operating to the northeast, at 0658hrs—sunrise—the six assigned F4F fighters began a scheduled 17-minute strafing of Wotje to suppress potential enemy air. Wotje's antiaircraft guns opened on *Enterprise*'s approaching fighters and then Spruance's spotting planes.

Spruance commenced his bombardment at 0715hrs. Ten minutes later the Japanese retaliated with their own fire, beginning from ships in the lagoon, but this was ineffective. At 0810hrs *Northampton* and *Salt Lake City* shifted fire from vessels afloat to Wotje targets

Rear Admiral Spruance's flagship, heavy cruiser *Northampton*, shells Wotje during the February 1 Marshalls–Gilberts raids. The underweight *Northampton* was one of the "eggshells with hammers" (treaty cruisers) commissioned during the 1930s. (NHHC NH 50943)

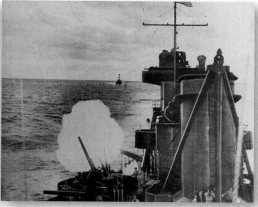

ashore. These were particularly well camouflaged, making gunnery difficult. Gasoline tanks were painted green and covered with sod, while other buildings were painted as if they were sand dunes; US gunners discovered many of them only because of their long morning shadows.

Japanese counterfire had been ineffective all morning, but at 0843hrs *Salt Lake City* was suddenly near-missed by several exploding shells; she increased speed and made evasive maneuvers just in time for two 5in. shells to detonate astern. Then, at 0848hrs, a Japanese salvo straddled *Northampton*. However, although Japanese guns continued firing another hour, their accuracy fell off again. After ceasing fire at 0853hrs, Spruance ordered his spotter planes to attack remaining targets with the two 100lb bombs that each carried.

At 1116hrs *Enterprise* launched a follow-up strike of eight SBDs and nine TBDs to finish off anything on Wotje that had survived Spruance's surface bombardment. Nearly ten tons of bombs from the 17 *Enterprise* bombers "completely destroyed" what remained of Wotje's airbase, while only two vessels were observed surviving in Wotje's harbor.

Halsey's attack on Taroa, February 1

Chester, *Balch*, and *Maury* were assigned to shell Taroa. *Chester*'s Captain Thomas M. Shock held overall command as senior officer present. Their assigned air support was Lieutenant James Gray's five Wildcats. *Chester* launched four floatplanes at 0600hrs, two each for spotting and for reconnaissance. An hour later two unidentified Japanese planes unsuccessfully attacked Shock's formation.

At 0710hrs two coast artillery batteries opened fire on *Chester*. Within five minutes Shock's own force opened its bombardment of Taroa. Meanwhile, Lieutenant James Gray's five Wildcats had misidentified the island of Tjan as their actual target of Taroa. Gray and his wingman had bombed it at 0700hrs before realizing their error and taking their charges southeast. Fifteen miles later, Gray's Wildcats reached the real Taroa and were shocked to find a large, well-stocked airbase. Those Wildcats that still had 100lb bombs dropped them, and then all five fighters made repeated strafing runs against the Japanese planes parked along the one-mile airstrip. Within minutes Taroa had scrambled seven A5M Claude fighters; the Americans shot down one but soon almost all the Wildcats' guns had jammed, a known and recurring problem. After an intense running dogfight, all five of Gray's Wildcats successfully escaped the aerial melee and headed back towards *Enterprise*.

USS *NORTHAMPTON* SHELLS WOTJE ISLAND, FEBRUARY 1, 1942 (PP.46–47)

On February 1, 1942, at around 0848hrs, the USS *Northampton* (**1**) began shelling Wotje Island. The heavy cruiser's 8in. guns (**2**), arranged in three 250-ton triple turrets, are aimed at Wotje, which lies beyond the horizon out of sight. The 8in./55-caliber gun formed the main battery of USN heavy cruisers. *Northampton* has already launched her spotter planes, which are looking out for enemy movements and spotting the fall of shot from her artillery. *Northampton* is being straddled by several large salvo splashes (**3**) from Japanese coastal artillery that have come uncomfortably close.

Northampton, the lead ship in her six-ship class, was named for the city of Northampton, Massachusetts. Commissioned in 1930, she was originally classified a light cruiser on account of her thin armor, but was later reclassified a heavy cruiser. *Northampton* would be struck by two "Long Lance" torpedoes from the Japanese destroyer *Oyashio* during the Battle of Tassafaronga on November 30, 1942, and would sink the following day.

After a half hour of US shelling, at 0740hrs at least eight bombers were seen taking off from Taroa. Captain Shock decided "a speedy retirement was now in order." From then on until 0900hrs, "many dive-bombing and strafing attacks were made on the group," with *Chester* the main target. Shock ordered personnel from *Chester*'s now-silent 8in. guns to go assist the antiaircraft batteries. Despite hard maneuvering, at 0821hrs *Chester* was hit by a single 134lb bomb, killing eight men and wounding 34. Then at 0841hrs, eight Nell bombers appeared overhead at 12,000ft and emptied their payloads, with the nearest 500lb bomb missing *Chester* 100 yards aft. After this bombing run, Japanese air attacks fell off.

By now Gray's returning Wildcat pilots had been debriefed aboard *Enterprise*. The sudden revelation of a major airbase at Taroa just 100nm southeast of *Enterprise* demanded attention. At 0930hrs *Enterprise* launched a follow-up Taroa strike of nine SBDs under Lieutenant-Commander William R. Hollingsworth. By the time this formation reached Taroa, most of the IJN fighters were back on the ground getting refueled and rearmed. The nine SBDs attacked Taroa's airfield and radio station with 500lb and 100lb bombs, recording substantial damage. Five A5M Claude fighters attacked Hollingsworth's bombers, but all nine SBDs successfully escaped back to *Enterprise*.

At 1030hrs *Enterprise* launched a third and final airstrike against Taroa. Led by Lieutenant-Commander Dick Best, these nine SBDs reached a point near Taroa and began their attack runs from 13,000ft. They were pursued by four Claude fighters. One Claude latched onto the tail of one of Best's SBDs and was subsequently shot down by the last SBD in formation. Best's planes dropped their bombs on aircraft hangars and several Nell bombers parked on the airfield. The SBDs were then immediately jumped by a low-level Japanese fighter patrol. Multiple dogfights broke out, in which the SBDs claimed two Claudes shot down. One SBD was seen fleeing into a cloud while chased by a Claude. It was never seen again.

Chester recovered her four floatplanes at 1130hrs and made a belated rendezvous with *Enterprise*; Shock's vessels had taken a roundabout route to avoid giving away *Enterprise*'s location to the Japanese aircraft. Captain Shock estimated that his force had destroyed several buildings and one observation tower, had started three or four fires (including an oil tank), had silenced four enemy gun shore batteries, and had damaged a radio tower. The *Enterprise* Air Group believed it had additionally destroyed two hangars and a radio station.

Halsey retires from the Marshalls, February 1

Enterprise's February 1 strike damaged IJN Sixth Fleet flagship light cruiser *Katori* (wounding Sixth Fleet commander Vice Admiral Mitsumi Shimizu), damaged the

Chester sailors inspect damage from the 134lb bomb that killed eight of their shipmates. *Chester* and her two escorting destroyers had the bad luck of being assigned to bombard Taroa, which unknown to the Americans possessed a very large and modern airbase. (US Navy)

Chester's senior aviator, Lieutenant Wilson R. Bartlett, has just returned from a shell-spotting mission over Taroa and is preparing to make his report. Behind him is the deck damage from the 134lb aerial bomb that hit *Chester*. (NHHC NH 50945)

11,930-ton submarine tender *Yasukuni Maru*, and damaged submarine *I-23*, as well as several other ships.

American naval historian John Lundstrom aptly described Halsey's February 1 performance: "For five hours he laid the *Enterprise* alongside Wotje much like an old-time frigate grappling an opponent." According to Halsey:

> Our surface bombardments were followed by a series of dive-bombing attacks. That day the *Enterprise* launched and landed twenty-one times. The pilots and crewmen would fly off and fight, fly back and take a breather while their planes were being refueled and rearmed, and then fly off and fight again. Three of these strikes were led by Lt. Comdr. William R. Hollingsworth, the skipper of Bombing 6. When he returned from the third, around 1300, he made his usual report to the bridge, then added, "Admiral, don't you think it's about time we got the hell out of here?"
>
> For nine hours we had been maneuvering the *Enterprise* in a rectangle only 5 miles by 20, so close to Wotje that my naked eye could see its AA bursting around our planes and—a more cordial sight—a column of smoke from the burning installations. We had been riding our luck hard enough; we had already dodged a periscope, and enemy planes were bound to pick up our trail soon.
>
> I told Hollingsworth, "My boy, I've been thinking the same thing myself!" And right there we formed a club that later achieved some notoriety. It was called "Haul Ass with Halsey."

Spruance's bombardment force successfully rendezvoused with *Enterprise* at 1230hrs. An hour later, five incoming bogies were detected on *Enterprise*'s radar. These were G3M Nell bombers, which quickly closed the range unmolested. Attacking from off *Enterprise*'s starboard bow, the five G3Ms each dropped a stick of three bombs. All missed, but the nearest detonated 30ft off *Enterprise*'s port side, shredding a fuel line. The resulting gasoline fire would ultimately be contained at the cost of one man dead.

As the five G3Ms sped away from *Enterprise*, one suddenly turned around, blazing, and commenced an apparent suicide run towards *Enterprise*. Diving through flak, the G3M appeared on a sure collision course for the carrier. Just then, Aviation Machinist's Mate 3rd Class Bruno Gaido ran across *Enterprise*'s deck, leapt into the rear cockpit of a parked SBD, and heroically poured 0.30-caliber fire into the diving G3M, which was deflected just enough to shear the tail off Gaido's SBD and harmlessly cartwheel into the sea mere yards away from *Enterprise*.

Later that afternoon, two more G3Ms attacked *Enterprise* but were shot down by the CAP and *Enterprise* antiaircraft fire. Within a few hours dusk had fallen, and *Enterprise* escaped into the night with only light damage. *Enterprise* shortly found a cold front, and TF-8 steamed northeast, out of danger. Halsey's

Browning 0.50-caliber antiaircraft guns aboard *Enterprise* open up against Japanese attackers on February 1, 1942. This appears to be the starboard side. An SBD Dauntless dive-bomber is parked on the flight deck above and behind the gunners. (NHHC NH 50935)

TF-8 had lost seven aircraft—five SBDs and one F4F from *Enterprise* and a *Salt Lake City* floatplane damaged beyond recovery and jettisoned. Total TF-8 casualties were 20 men killed and missing (11 airmen) and 44 wounded (four airmen).

Fletcher strikes Jaluit, Makin, and Mili, February 1

In contrast to TF-8's Halsey, who had had *Enterprise* steam virtually in sight of his targets and repeatedly pound them over the course of several hours, accompanied by surface shelling, Fletcher's TF-17 plan to the south involved two sequential deckload strikes off *Yorktown*, followed by a hasty break for the proverbial exits.

By the night of January 31, *Yorktown* and heavy cruisers *Louisville* and *Astoria* found themselves steaming due west at 25.5 knots. Following behind *Yorktown* and the cruisers at 15 knots were TF-17's four escorting destroyers. Understrength at just 60 operational aircraft, *Yorktown* approached her designated launch point midway between the Marshalls and Gilberts.

At 0500hrs *Yorktown* and her two cruisers abruptly reversed course, and at 0517hrs *Yorktown* began launching her deckload of 17 SBDs and 11 TBDs towards Jaluit. *Yorktown* was then 140nm from Jaluit, 127nm north of Makin, and 71nm south of Mili. Once the Jaluit strike had cleared the flight deck, the deck was re-spotted with 14 SBD-5s from VS-5, each armed with a 500lb bomb. Destined for Makin and Mili, this second deckload began launching at 0544hrs.

Cruising beneath a rain squall at an altitude of 1,000ft, the nine SBDs assigned to hit Makin sighted their target at 0630hrs. After climbing to an attack altitude of 12,000ft, the SBDs observed a "seaplane tender" and two four-engined seaplanes anchored in the lagoon. The Americans launched their dive-bombing attack at 0658hrs. One bomb hit the "seaplane tender," which was actually the 2,900-ton armed transport *Nagata Maru*, inflicting what the Japanese described as "medium damage." After the dive-bombing attack, the SBDs strafed the two seaplanes, leaving them burning.

Meanwhile, the five SBDs assigned to bomb Mili found nothing on the island of any value to attack, and all 14 SBDs returned without incident to *Yorktown*. They were shortly re-launched to bolster *Yorktown*'s low-altitude CAP.

Commander Curtis Smiley was to lead the Jaluit strike group of 17 SBDs and 11 TBDs. Visibly hovering between *Yorktown* and Jaluit to the northwest were dark, heavy cloud banks and flashing lighting. In the dark, nearly moonless early morning the 28 bombers were unable to properly assemble near the carrier. After considerable confusion, Lieutenant-Commander Robert Armstrong led about 22 aircraft towards Jaluit, departing some 20 minutes late. However, even these aircraft soon got separated in the storm.

The few *Yorktown* planes to reach Jaluit began arriving at 0700hrs. Over the course of a half hour, they attacked in bedraggled groups of two and three aircraft at a time. Jaluit itself was completely covered in fierce thunderstorms. The low, thick cloud cover forced the *Yorktown* bombers to make their runs from low altitude. The first Dauntless to attack scored the Jaluit raid's only clear hit, a bomb on 8,600-ton transport *Kanto Maru*, causing light damage. Some planes dropped their bombs on shore, while others strafed light craft in the lagoon. Only about 15 SBDs and six TBDs are believed to have actually attacked Jaluit. The poor weather meant there

AMM3/C BRUNO GAIDO DOWNS LIEUTENANT KAZUO NAKAI'S MITSUBISHI G3M BOMBER AS IT ATTACKS USS *ENTERPRISE* (PP.52–53)

On 1 February 1942, five Japanese G3M twin-engined bombers made it through *Enterprise*'s CAP (fighter) defenses following the US carrier raid on the Japanese-held Marshall Islands. All the bombers missed and turned away, except the badly damaged lead plane, piloted by Lieutenant Kazuo Nakai, which turned back in an attempt to crash on the *Enterprise*.

As the aircraft neared the ship and antiaircraft fire seemed ineffective, Aviation Machinist Mate 3rd Class (AMM3/C) Bruno Gaido leaped out of the catwalk, climbed into the rear seat of a parked SBD Dauntless dive-bomber (his normal position as radioman–gunner when the plane was airborne), swiveled the plane's aft twin .30-caliber machine guns, and opened fire. While standing, he poured accurate fire into the low-flying bomber's cockpit, causing it to lose control. In this scene, we see the Japanese bomber (**1**) barely missing the flight deck, its wingtip cutting the tail off the SBD Dauntless dive-bomber Gaido is in (**2**). The impact will cause the parked aircraft to spin round. Gaido continued firing on the bomber throughout, until it crashed in the water on the opposite side of the ship.

were virtually no Japanese aircraft airborne to oppose the Americans. Nevertheless, six *Yorktown* planes and their crews were lost, with Lieutenant Harlan Anderson radioing that he and another plane were having to put down alongside of one of Jaluit's northwestern islands.

By 0930hrs the weather over *Yorktown* had become so unfriendly that Fletcher recovered his full CAP. *Yorktown* began landing her Jaluit strike in 50-knot wind gusts and rain so intense it cut visibility to 100 yards. Several US planes returned from Jaluit with less than two gallons of fuel remaining.

A US destroyer from Fletcher's Task Force 17 prepares to pick up the crew of a downed SBD Dauntless from *Yorktown*, February 1, 1942. The Dauntless appears to have ditched nearby after making its attack on Makin. (US Navy).

Just after 1000hrs Fletcher dispatched destroyers *Russell*, *Hughes*, and *Sims* 15–20nm astern of TF-17 to guide *Yorktown* pilots home and help rescue anyone who had to ditch.

However, unknown to the Americans, *Yorktown*'s strike on Jaluit had missed three H6K Mavis flying boats in the harbor. After the strike concluded, these planes took off in pursuit of the US carrier that had attacked them. At 1109hrs an H6K burst out of the clouds and began an attack against destroyer *Russell*, which responded with 5in. antiaircraft fire. The flying boat broke off before dropping four bombs at *Sims*, all of which missed astern.

At 1313hrs a Mavis flying boat out of Jaluit suddenly appeared ten miles ahead of *Yorktown*, which vectored two Wildcats to intercept. They shot it down within four minutes, with one of the Wildcat pilots blurting excitedly over the radio, "We shot his ass off!" As the stricken Mavis tumbled in flames in full view of the American sailors, *Yorktown*'s fiery executive officer, Commander J.J. "Jocko" Clark, grabbed a bullhorn and shouted over the carrier's loudspeakers: "Burn, you son-of-a-bitch, burn!" Fletcher's force ultimately escaped the Marshalls–Gilberts raids having lost a total of eight aircraft, including an SOC Seagull floatplane from cruiser *Louisville* which disappeared.

Results from the Marshalls–Gilberts raids

The two US carriers had lost a combined total of 12 planes during the Marshalls–Gilberts raids. Reports of the exact damage to the Japanese vary considerably. However, it appears combined Japanese losses were nine planes destroyed on the ground, three A5M fighters shot down, and subchaser *Shonan Maru No. 10* sunk. Numerous small craft appear also to have been sunk. However, a considerable number of facilities and ships were damaged, some seriously. Ninety Japanese were killed, including IJN 6th Base Force commander Rear Admiral Yukicki Yashiro, the first Japanese admiral killed in action during the Pacific War.

Japanese radio propaganda scoffed that the US raids were mere "aerial guerilla warfare." Confiding to his diary, Yamamoto's Combined Fleet chief-of-staff Rear Admiral Matome Ugaki gasped, "[So] they have come after all!" and admitted the US raids were "a reproach that went to the heart." Indeed, Ugaki claimed, it had been two months since Pearl Harbor—time enough for the USN to regroup. Ugaki felt the IJN should have expected a counterattack from the Americans, especially as "Adventure is one of their characteristics." However, Ugaki expressed relief the Americans had merely "given us a good lesson" with a relatively inconsequential raid, rather

A Curtiss SOC Seagull floatplane, probably from *Northampton*, soars over a burning Wotje after the island was bombarded by *Enterprise* aircraft and two of the carrier's escorting heavy cruisers. The floatplane's mission was shell-spotting and observation. (NHHC NH 97593)

Vice Admiral Bill Halsey, Rear Admiral Spruance, Rear Admiral Aubrey Fitch, and one unidentified officer congratulate each other aboard *Enterprise* shortly after the task force returned to Pearl Harbor on February 5, 1942. (NHHC 80-G-63338-B)

than directly attacking Tokyo. Nevertheless, "our carelessness in being ignorant of the enemy approach until he was so close was extremely regrettable … After experiencing defensive weakness ourselves, we cannot laugh at the enemy's confusion at the time of the surprise attack at Pearl Harbor."

Halsey's autobiography recalled:

When we reentered on February 5, flying our largest colors, such a roar went up that Kailua must have heard it, across the island. The ships in the harbor blew their sirens, the crews yelled, and the troops at Hickam Field cheered us all the way to our mooring (cheering a ship in is a custom of the Royal Navy; I had never heard it in ours before). The men of the task force tried to cheer back but choked up. I myself cried and was not ashamed. … Chester Nimitz was down at the dock. He didn't wait for the *Enterprise* to lower a gangway; he came over the side in a bo's'n's chair and, pumping my hand, told me, "Nice going!" … After him came COMDESPAC, Rear Admiral Robert A. Theobald, who shook his finger in my face and shouted, "Damn you, Bill, you've got no business getting home from that one. No business at all!"

The reason we brought off these early raids is that we violated all the rules and traditions of naval warfare. We did the exact opposite of what the enemy expected. We did not keep our carriers behind the battle; we deliberately exposed them to shore-based planes. Most important, whatever we did, we did fast. I have heard that there was a popular saying on the *Enterprise* at this time, "The Admiral will get us in, and the Captain will get us out."

Halsey offered a keen assessment of the February 1 raids:

When the profit of the two forces is added, the total is not spectacular … [but] although it was barren in physical spoils, it was rich in Intelligence material—we had discovered operational airfields on Roi, Taroa, and Wotje—and richer still in morale. We had been whipped in the attack that opened the war and had been on the defensive ever since. When our task forces sortied for the Marshalls raid, you could almost smell the defeatism around Pearl. Now the offensive spirit was reestablished; officers and men were bushy-tailed again. So, presently, was the American public. At last we had been able to answer their roweling question, "Where is the Navy?" … It was the Pacific Fleet, the big fleet, the fleet maimed at Pearl Harbor, that had now paid the first installment on its bill.

On February 13, the notoriously media-averse USN released details of the Marshalls–Gilberts raids to the American public. The highly quotable but previously obscure Halsey immediately became an American popular culture celebrity. In contrast to the typically elitist, aristocratic, and enigmatic

USN officer culture, the simple and straightforward Halsey was a US admiral who could be readily understood and embraced by the American mass public. More importantly, Halsey was now a proven fighter and winner at a time when America desperately needed a hero.

US PACIFIC FLEET STRATEGY, FEBRUARY 1942

The Pacific Fleet was unable to counterattack against overwhelming Japanese superiority in the ABDA and Philippines areas. However, responding to the Japanese capture of Rabaul, on January 24 King proposed a new Pacific naval command to the east of Australia. This new theater, called the ANZAC Area, would be officially activated on February 7 and remain outside Nimitz's jurisdiction. For its commander, King selected former TF-14 skipper Herbert Leary, who was promoted to vice admiral. Although commanded by an American, ANZAC's primary naval power would be Rear Admiral John G. Crace's Australian Squadron, which was renamed the ANZAC Squadron.

Meanwhile the overall strategic plan regarding the delicate balance between Australia and the Central Pacific remained unresolved. If the Pacific Fleet committed all its resources to reinforcing the long Australia lifeline, this would leave the Central Pacific open to Japanese attack. The second option, greatly favored by Nimitz's planners, was to leave strength in the Central Pacific, and undertake "bold operations" in that theater when the situation presented itself. Prodded by King, on February 5, Pacific Fleet planners proposed a combined carrier–battleship strike against Truk.

Obsessed with reinforcing the South Pacific, on February 6 King directly ordered TF-11, Brown's *Lexington* task force, south to the new ANZAC area, out of Nimitz's direct command. TF-11 would join Crace's ANZAC Squadron and be additionally reinforced by heavy cruisers *Pensacola* and *San Francisco*, plus six destroyers, all recently released from convoy escort duty. King then ordered Nimitz to support TF-11 with "all practical" patrol planes and heavy bombers he could spare from his own command. For his part, Brown felt that sending TF-11 deep into the South Pacific, thousands of miles from any repair facilities, was like "jumping out into space."

With his Central Pacific forces suddenly gutted, on February 7 Nimitz recommended to King that carrier raids be temporarily suspended. King refused to suspend opportunistic raids, and on February 9, King ordered Nimitz to maintain "a continuous effort to damage ships and bases." However, the Pacific Fleet was already understrength and constant detachments of cruisers, destroyers, and auxiliaries were required to support US convoys headed to the South Pacific. Under these circumstances, planning diversionary attacks strong enough to substantially influence the Japanese without being unduly risky proved difficult; Nimitz's staff debated raids against Wake, Eniwetok, Rabaul, and even the Japanese capital.

JAPANESE CARRIER ACTIONS, FEBRUARY 1–19, 1942

On February 1 the Combined Fleet abruptly canceled plans to move against Celebes. Instead, *Akagi*, *Kaga*, and *Zuikaku* sortied from Truk due east at

Port Darwin, Australia burns after the Japanese carrier raid. A US destroyer is prominent in the foreground. The Port Darwin raid was impressive but probably a waste of powerful Japanese carrier assets. Commander Mitsuo Fuchida and his fellow airmen would have much preferred to have struck Pearl Harbor a second time. (Keystone/Hulton Archive/Getty Images)

top speed to hunt down and destroy the unidentified US carrier that had hit the Marshalls hours earlier. Fuchida recalled:

> The impulsive action really made little sense. It would take us two full days to cover the 1,200nm distance from Truk to the Marshalls, and in that interval the enemy was sure to retire to safety. Nevertheless, I inwardly rejoiced. Futile as it seemed, I thought our mad dash might just be the gesture that was needed to persuade Combined Fleet to re-direct the Nagumo Force eastward against its logical and potentially most dangerous opponent, the U.S. carrier force.

Additionally, Rear Admiral Aritomo Goto's heavy cruisers, Cruiser Division 6, sortied to engage the Americans. Light carrier *Shoho*, just recently administratively assigned to Fourth Fleet, was to rendezvous with Goto at sea. Fourth Fleet's submarines also sortied from Kwajalein to intercept the Americans. However, the IJN's entire multi-headed pursuit was canceled the following day. *Akagi*, *Kaga*, and *Zuikaku* were ordered to Palau, where they arrived on February 8.

In response to the Marshalls and Gilberts raids, Yamamoto detached the 5th Carrier Division (fleet carriers *Shokaku* and *Zuikaku*) from Truk to Home Islands waters to defensively patrol the homeland. Yamamoto, overreacting to the ultimately minor February 1 raids, had at a stroke removed one-third of the Combined Fleet's striking power from the war. For the next six weeks *Shokaku* and *Zuikaku* would remain off Japan on useless defensive patrols, burning fuel and accomplishing nothing.

Akagi's Commander Fuchida excoriated Combined Fleet's response to the raids, which was both to downplay their significance, and to harshly criticize the isolated outposts for being taken by surprise at all. But worst of all, the Combined Fleet:

> … failed on its own part to produce any positive and effective plan for dealing with the enemy carrier force. Instead, it took a feeble and purely negative countermeasure which struck me as worse than no action at all.

This countermeasure was an order for Carrier Division 5 (*Zuikaku*, *Shokaku*) from the Nagumo Force to carry out defensive air patrols east of the homeland. It sprang from Combined Fleet apprehension that the enemy, having directed a successful strike against the Marshalls, might be emboldened to attempt similar strikes against objectives closer to Japan—conceivably even the Imperial capital itself! The detachment of the two fleet carriers for patrol duty was designed only to guard against this worst eventuality. Unfortunately, its effect was to dissipate the strength of the one Japanese force which, with all six of its carriers operating together, could have confidently taken the offensive against any enemy in the Pacific, including the undamaged American carrier force.

Combined Fleet strongly wished to neutralize Allied bases in northwest Australia that could potentially interfere with Japanese operations in the Netherlands East Indies. Combined Fleet proposed an amphibious invasion of Port Darwin, Australia, which the Naval General Staff and the IJA summarily dismissed. Combined Fleet settled on a devastating Kido Butai strike to destroy Port Darwin's potential as a base. With *Zuikaku* and *Shokaku* detached on defensive patrol of the Home Islands, Vice Admiral Nagumo was temporarily down to only *Akagi* and *Kaga*, but he would be reinforced at Palau by Rear Admiral Yamaguchi's *Soryu* and *Hiryu*, which had been operating independently since December 16.

Led by Nagumo, on February 15, carriers *Akagi*, *Kaga*, *Soryu*, and *Hiryu*, battleships *Hiei* and *Kirishima*, heavy cruisers *Tone* and *Chikuma*, light cruiser *Abukuma*, and eight destroyers sortied from Palau. The morning of February 19 Nagumo's four carriers launched 188 planes against Port Darwin. The Japanese raid sank eight ships, including destroyer USS *Peary* (DD-226) and US Army transport *General M.C. Meigs* (AP-116). Another nine ships were damaged including seaplane tender USS *William B. Preston* (AVD-7). Fifteen planes were also destroyed, including nine Curtiss P-40E Warhawk fighters. Although Fuchida personally led the strike, he questioned its utility. "As at Rabaul," Fuchida recalled, "the job to be done seemed hardly worthy of the Nagumo Force."

ACTION OFF BOUGAINVILLE, FEBRUARY 20, 1942

Vice Admiral Wilson Brown's TF-11 comprised fast carrier *Lexington*, as well as heavy cruisers *Minneapolis*, *Indianapolis*, *Pensacola*, and *San Francisco*, plus ten destroyers. TF-11 had sortied from Oahu on January 31, and by February 10 had passed into the jurisdiction of Commander ANZAC Forces, Vice Admiral Herbert Leary. King immediately ordered Brown and Leary to conduct offensive operations. Brown duly formulated a plan for a combined air–surface bombardment of Rabaul, to be coordinated with USAAF heavy bombers to simultaneously hit Rabaul at sunrise, February 21. King and Leary both approved, and ordered by King, Nimitz dispatched 12 USAAF B-17 heavy bombers to Townsville in northeast Australia, in range of Rabaul. Seaplane tender *Curtiss* (AV-4) and her six PBY-5 flying boats were simultaneously deployed to Nouméa in New Caledonia.

After the Americans' February 1 raids, Japanese officials in the Rabaul and Mandates area were nervous, as IGHQ had intercepted heavy American radio traffic emanating from near Hawaii. On February 14 the Japanese went

The battle off Bougainville, February 19–22, 1942

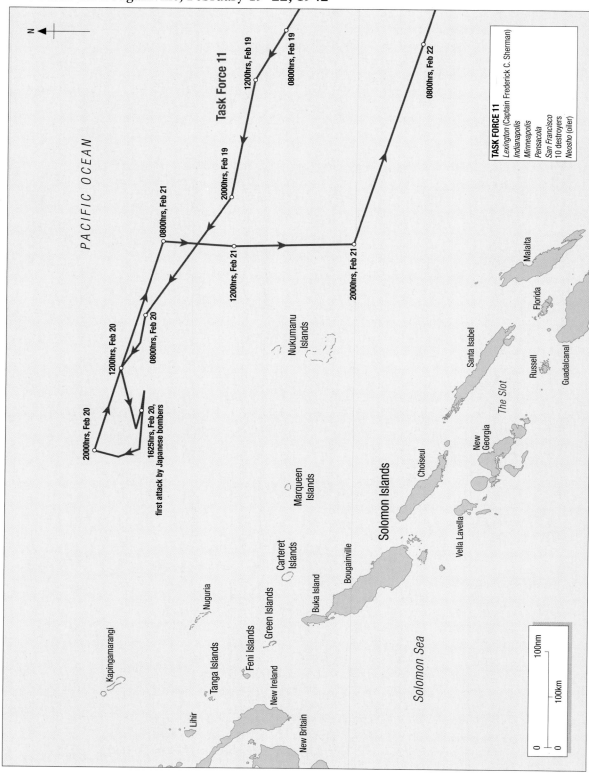

N

PACIFIC OCEAN

Task Force 11

0800hrs, Feb 19
1200hrs, Feb 19
2000hrs, Feb 19

0800hrs, Feb 22

0800hrs, Feb 21

1200hrs, Feb 21

2000hrs, Feb 21

0800hrs, Feb 20

1200hrs, Feb 20

2000hrs, Feb 20

1625hrs, Feb 20,
first attack by Japanese bombers

Nukumanu
Islands

Marqueen
Islands

Carteret
Islands

Green Islands

Feni Islands

Tanga Islands

Nuguria

Kapingamarangi

Lihir

New Ireland

New Britain

Buka Island

Bougainville

Solomon Islands

Choiseul

Vella Lavella

New
Georgia

The Slot

Santa Isabel

Russell

Malaita

Florida

Guadalcanal

Solomon Sea

TASK FORCE 11
Lexington (Captain Frederick C. Sherman)
Indianapolis
Minneapolis
Pensacola
San Francisco
10 destroyers
Neosho (oiler)

0   100nm
0   100km

A modern view of Simpson Harbour and Rabaul, from the Vulcanology Observatory. The original town of Rabaul, to the left of the photograph, was destroyed in a volcano eruption in 1937, killing over 500 people. Rabaul's Simpson Harbour, however, is one of the finest anchorages in the world. (Public Domain)

on alert. Five days later a Japanese island facility 160nm southwest of Truk inexplicably reported two US destroyers. Although this was a false report, it inspired Rabaul to announce an alert for February 20, when four H6K4 Mavis flying boats would patrol an easterly pie slice over the Americans' expected approach out to a range of 500nm. Additional reconnaissance sorties would emanate from Truk and the Marshalls.

Patiently waiting for contact reports would be Japanese combat aircraft based at Rabaul and the Mandates. The 4th Kokutai had only just been established in the Rabaul area on February 10 and was understrength. Its 16 A5M4 Claude and ten A6M2 Zero fighters were based at Rabaul, while the 4th Kokutai's 18 G4M1 Betty bombers were deployed at the nearby Vunakanau airfield. At Rabaul's Simpson Harbour were a handful of H6K4 Mavis flying boats of the Yokohama Kokutai, specially trained for night torpedo attacks. Deployed farther afield, the Chitose Kokutai had an additional nine G4M1 bombers on hand at Truk, plus another 27 G4M1 bombers and 36 fighters stationed in the Marshalls.

Brown's carrier force steamed west-northwest at 15 knots; Brown planned on approaching Rabaul from the northeast and to hit it with an airstrike at sunrise February 21, followed by a possible surface bombardment. At daybreak, February 20, *Lexington* launched six SBD Dauntlesses of VS-2 on a search out to 300nm ahead of TF-11. By 1000hrs *Lexington*'s CXAM-1 air search radar detected the Dauntlesses returning; *Lexington*'s first six-fighter CAP would launch immediately after they were recovered. At 1015hrs *Lexington*'s CXAM-1 detected what appeared to be a new bogey at 35nm, bearing 180 degrees. Captain Ted Sherman scrambled six F4F Wildcat fighters to intercept under Lieutenant-Commander Jimmy Thach.

From Rabaul, Goto had launched three H6K4s at sunrise to scout to the east. At 1030hrs the H6K4 flown by Lieutenant Junior-Grade Noboru Sakai reported sighting an enemy force east-northeast of Rabaul at a range of 450nm.

Guided by *Lexington*'s Fighter Direction Officer (FDO), Thach and his wingman Ensign Edward Sellstrom searched for the bogey. After the FDO directed Thach and Sellstrom directly into a rain squall, the flying boat suddenly loomed out of the clouds "right into my lap," as Thach later described. For several minutes Sakai skillfully evaded the Americans in the

ACTION OFF BOUGAINVILLE ORDER OF BATTLE, FEBRUARY 20, 1942

IJN ORDER OF BATTLE
FOURTH FLEET—VICE ADMIRAL SHIGEYOSHI INOUE
6th Cruiser Division (Truk)—Rear Admiral Aritomo Goto
    Heavy cruiser *Aoba*
    Heavy cruiser *Kako*
    Heavy cruiser *Kinugasa*
    Heavy cruiser *Furutaka*
18th Cruiser Division (Truk)—Rear Admiral Kuninori Marumo
    Light cruiser *Tenryu*
    Light cruiser *Tatsuta*
24th Air Flotilla (Rabaul)—Rear Admiral Eiji Goto
    4th Kokutai
        Vunakanau—18 x G4M1 Betty bombers (551lb bombs only)
        Rabaul—16 x A5M4 Claude carrier fighters
        Rabaul—10 x A6M2 Zeke (Zero) carrier fighters
    Yokohama Kokutai
        24 x H6K4 Mavis flying boats
    Chitose Kokutai
        Truk—9 x G4M1 Betty bombers
        Marshalls—27 x G4M1 Betty bombers
        Marshalls—36 x fighters

USN ORDER OF BATTLE
TASK FORCE 11—VICE ADMIRAL WILSON BROWN (*LEXINGTON*)
CV-2 *Lexington*—Captain Frederick C. "Ted" Sherman
    Lexington Air Group—Commander Bill Ault
        VF-3—Lieutenant-Commander Jimmy Thach
        VS-2—Lieutenant-Commander Robert Dixon
        VB-2—Lieutenant-Commander Weldon Hamilton
        VT-2—Lieutenant-Commander Jimmy Brett
CA-24 *Pensacola*—Captain Frank L. Lowe
CA-35 *Indianapolis*—Captain Edward W. Hanson
CA-36 *Minneapolis*—Captain Frank J. Lowry
CA-38 *San Francisco*—Captain Daniel J. Callaghan
DD-349 *Dewey*—Lieutenant-Commander Charles F. Chillingsworth
DD-350 *Hull*—Lieutenant-Commander Richard F. Stout
DD-351 *MacDonough*—Lieutenant-Commander John M. McIsaac
DD-353 *Dale*—Lieutenant-Commander Anthony L. Rorschach
DD-355 *Aylwin*—Lieutenant-Commander Robert H. Rogers
DD-360 *Phelps*—Lieutenant-Commander Edward L. Beck
DD-361 *Clark*—Commander Myron T. Richardson
DD-366 *Drayton*—Lieutenant-Commander Laurence A. Abercrombie
DD-386 *Bagley*—Lieutenant-Commander George A. Sinclair
DD-392 *Patterson*—Commander Frank R. Walker

clouds, before bursting into the open at 1,000ft altitude. As Sakai's tail gunner fired 20mm rounds at Sellstrom, the Wildcats made two strafing runs on the flying boat. Sakai's Mavis burst into flames and crashed into the sea at 1112hrs, with *Lexington*'s men cheering the smoke plume visible on the horizon.

Within minutes, *Lexington*'s CXAM-1 had detected a second bogey. Lieutenant Junior-Grade Burt Stanley and his wingman Ensign Leon Haynes were directed to intercept the unknown aircraft. This was Warrant Officer Kiyoshi Hayashi's Mavis on patrol out of Rabaul, a fourth flying boat which had been dispatched at 0800hrs on its own easterly sector. Sakai had made his initial report while Hayashi's Mavis was still outbound, and Hayashi was promptly redirected to *Lexington*'s reported location.

After being directed north 20nm, Stanley and Haynes found Hayashi's Mavis. "Tally-ho from Orange Leader," called Haynes, "A big four-engined patrol plane." Hayashi's Mavis soon spotted the two Wildcats maneuvering into attack position. Hayashi dropped his bombs to flee, and the Mavis' defensive guns opened up on the Americans. Stanley and Haynes methodically worked over the Mavis until it crashed flaming into the sea, its resulting smoke plume visible from TF-11. Ruminating later to his diary, Stanley acknowledged: "Ten men were dead and the plane, efforts of a hundred, was destroyed. But it had to be."

Nevertheless, it was obvious the Japanese were aware a US carrier task force was bearing down on Rabaul. Brown's *Lexington* strike would not hit Rabaul until the following morning, giving the Rabaul authorities 20 hours to evacuate the harbor, ready defensive measures, bring aerial reinforcements in from

Carrier *Lexington* underway in October 1941. She has just departed San Diego. Note the false bow wave and the F2A Buffalo fighters. The Buffaloes would not be exchanged for Wildcats until several months into the war. They only saw minor action in USN service. (US Navy via Navsource)

Truk and the Marshalls, and of course launch pre-emptive air strikes against the *Lexington* task force. Additionally, low wind conditions had thus far caused TF-11 to consume more fuel than expected to conduct flight operations. Brown no longer had a safe fuel margin to conduct high-speed operations in the event of a battle with the Japanese, and the nearest oiler rendezvous would be four days away on February 24. For Brown the only option was obvious, and despite the vigorous protestations of *Lexington*'s Captain Sherman, by noon Brown ordered the Rabaul strike canceled.

An F4F-3 Wildcat fighter on what appears to be a training mission. The dazzling US roundels and rudder stripes immediately identify the period as early 1942, but were considered to make US planes too easy a target. The red color also attracted friendly fire. By late spring 1942 all traces of red were removed from US aircraft. (Public Domain)

However, Brown could still feint aggressively toward Rabaul the rest of the afternoon, an action he hoped would yet accomplish the mission's strategic objective of diverting Japanese resources from the beleaguered Netherlands East Indies. Brown therefore prematurely executed TF-11's originally planned southwest turn towards Rabaul. Although Brown anticipated having to fight off bomber attacks, by 1330hrs *Lexington* and her escorts were bearing down directly on Rabaul. Brown then broke radio silence to report his altered course of action to Leary and King.

Meanwhile Rear Admiral Eiji Goto, 24th Air Flotilla commander, had correctly deduced the now-aborted US strategy of striking Rabaul at dawn the following morning. Of Rabaul's assigned 27 G4M Betty bombers, nine were still training at Tinian. Although Goto had 26 fighters available at Rabaul, 16 were the obsolescent A5M4 Claude, with a range of only 250nm. Goto did have ten ostensibly long-ranged, high performance A6M2 Zero fighters, but their drop tanks had not yet been delivered. Nor had any aerial torpedoes been delivered to Vunakanau airfield, where Rabaul's Betty bombers were deployed.

Japan's unexpectedly heavy initial air losses and lackadaisical production and administration meant that four weeks after its capture the IJN had only mustered 18 G4M bombers at Rabaul, no aerial torpedoes, and no drop tanks for its long-ranged Zero fighters. This was when Rabaul was intended to be Japan's most powerful and important South Pacific base.

By afternoon, February 20, Goto's Betty and Mavis bombers could already reach Brown's TF-11, but Goto's fighters—the Claudes and the drop tank-lacking Zeros—could not. Accordingly, several of Goto's staff urged Goto to wait until the following day to launch a properly escorted strike, but Goto chose to attack TF-11 immediately, even though it meant attacking without fighter escort. At 1310hrs Goto ordered his 4th Kokutai G4M Betty bombers to sortie from Rabaul against the oncoming US carrier.

Goto's 18 G4M crews were handpicked combat veterans who had already seen action in the Philippines and the Netherlands East Indies. Lacking torpedoes, the G4Ms would be loaded with two 551lb bombs each and forced to make horizontal bombing runs. However, torpedoes had been delivered to the Simpson Harbor seaplane base, allowing Goto to plan overnight torpedo attacks by his H6K4 Mavis flying boats.

Meanwhile, at 1400hrs a single H6K4, flown by Ensign Motohiro Makino, took off from Rabaul's Simpson Harbor. Makino's mission was to reestablish contact with the US task force and shadow it. Twenty minutes later, at 1420hrs, all 17 of Rabaul's operational G4M bombers (one was unavailable with mechanical problems) took off from Rabaul's Vunakanau airstrip and headed towards the Americans. The 17-bomber strike was commanded by Lieutenant-Commander Takuzo Ito. However, heavy clouds and occasional squalls east of Rabaul shortly forced Ito to divide his 17-bomber strike into two separate *chutai* (flights) to search for the US task force.

At 1542hrs, *Lexington*'s air search radar made an aerial contact due west at a range of 76nm, speed 150 knots, and an altitude of 8,000ft; however, the contact shortly faded. At 1615hrs *Lexington* launched her next six-fighter CAP shift early, to replace the current CAP, which was low on fuel. *Lexington*'s intermittent radar contact picked up for good at 1625hrs and in just three minutes the radar contact had closed to 24nm.

Flying at 11,000ft, the nine Betty bombers under Lieutenant Masayoshi Nakagawa sighted TF-11 and transmitted a contact report at 1635hrs. Moments later, the first two F4F Wildcats dove on the Japanese formation. They were soon joined by their four squadronmates. Nakagawa's bombers returned fire, but without escort the Wildcats began shooting them down in methodical passes, claiming four G4Ms inbound to TF-11.

Lexington made flank speed, but she had 14 fully fueled aircraft spotted forward, a serious danger during an attack. *Lexington*'s air officer, Commander Herbert Duckworth, ordered all 14 planes pushed to the stern and launched. "That re-spot was the fastest re-spot ever made in history," Duckworth recalled. "It was as if some great hand moved all the planes aft simultaneously." The running aerial battle was now within full view of TF-11, allowing the Americans to nervously watch the Japanese close towards them. By 1646hrs *Lexington* had cleared her deck of aircraft and opened fire, beginning evasive maneuvers. The five surviving G4M1s dropped their bombs, but all missed by 3,000 yards.

However, *Lexington* lookouts shortly spotted a damaged G4M1 bomber coming in low off the starboard bow, clearly intending to crash-dive; the suicide attacker was actually Nakagawa. *Lexington*'s starboard 1.1in. and 0.50-caliber guns opened up at a range of 2,500 yards, drawing visible smoke from Nakagawa's bomber at 1,000 yards. Moments later, at 1651hrs, the crippled Betty exploded in the water 75 yards astern the hard-turning *Lexington*. Brown was disconcerted by what he considered his men's overly jubilant cheering at every perceived Japanese reverse: "I even had to remind some members of my staff that this was not a football game."

Nevertheless, the pursuing Americans continued picking off the surviving Japanese, with an SBD splashing the last Betty some 80nm west of *Lexington*. All nine G4M1s of Nakagawa's formation had been shot down. Before they were annihilated, the fleeing Betty bombers managed to claim two US fighters, including Lieutenant Junior-Grade Howard Johnson, who managed to safely bail out. Minutes later, lookouts aboard destroyer *Patterson* spotted the second wave of inbound G4M1 bombers while *Patterson* was rescuing the downed Johnson. *Patterson* duly warned *Lexington* before finishing her rescue, a sailor recalling, "The smile on the pilot's face was a thing to remember."

The second Japanese attack of eight Betty bombers was led by Lieutenant-Commander Takuzo Ito, the overall Japanese strike commander. This group caught the inexperienced Americans almost entirely out of position, being detected only 12nm from *Lexington* and from the opposite side of TF-11. Only two Wildcats led by Lieutenant Butch O'Hare were available to intercept. However, O'Hare's wingman soon fell behind, leaving O'Hare to take them alone. Over the course of four minutes, the lone O'Hare employed methodical attack runs and seemingly shot down five bombers on his own. In fact, postwar research revealed that O'Hare had destroyed three bombers and turned two back, heavily damaged. O'Hare was ultimately credited with five kills, making him the USN's first official ace of World War II.

Regardless, O'Hare may have single-handedly saved *Lexington*. Only six bombers reached the carrier to strike it, with the nearest bomb missing *Lexington* astern by a mere 100ft. Like Nakagawa's bomber before him, Ito's Betty received mortal damage and turned around to crash-dive the carrier. Turning hard, *Lexington* poured antiaircraft fire into Ito's plane, which slammed into the ocean 1,500 yards ahead of *Lexington*. Several of Ito's surviving bombers were then shot down by F4Fs and SBDs on the way back to Rabaul. Just two bombers landed intact, both severely damaged, while a third bomber ditched in Simpson Harbour. The February 20 air battle off Bougainville had cost *Lexington* two fighters and one pilot. When including Nakagawa's flight, Brown's TF-11 had destroyed a grand total of 15 of 17 Betty bombers sent to attack them.

To continue bluffing the Japanese, Brown maintained *Lexington* on a direct course for Rabaul throughout daylight, then abruptly retired as night fell. With the omniscient gift of hindsight, one can now appreciate the irony of Brown's course of action. As it turned out, Brown had intentionally endured (and ultimately destroyed) a major Japanese bomber strike purely for appearances' sake, while—specifically to avoid damage to TF-11—Brown had simultaneously canceled his own actual chance to damage Rabaul itself. This was exactly when Brown had unknowingly wrecked Rabaul's immediate ability to harm his own force. Nevertheless, ready IJN reinforcements were in the area, and under the intelligence available to him in the moment, Brown's decision was perfectly reasonable.

More importantly, Brown's intuition was essentially correct. Still attempting to find the encroaching US carrier, six torpedo-armed Mavis flying boats would launch from

Lieutenant Edward "Butch" O'Hare in a publicity shot some time after his feat off Bougainville. Despite the heroic pose, O'Hare was personally modest and shy. He begged his commanding officers to not recommend him for the Medal of Honor. O'Hare died under mysterious circumstances the night of November 26, 1943 while leading an experimental night interception mission. (NHHC 80-G-K-892-B)

Rabaul in the early dark of February 21. They returned empty-handed after sun-up, but with daylight breaking additional Japanese planes began fanning out from Rabaul and Truk in a justified but equally fruitless search for the long-gone *Lexington*.

Echoing the IJN's overwrought response to the Marshalls–Gilberts raids, Vice Admiral Inoue had sortied his major Fourth Fleet surface assets from Truk and Rabaul, including his four heavy cruisers, two light cruisers, and their escorting destroyers, with Rear Admiral Goto anticipating a planned February 21 night surface action against the presumably still approaching TF-11. Additionally, light carrier *Shoho*, on ferry duty to Palau, was ordered to turn around, while Yamamoto dispatched air units to Truk from as far away as the Netherlands East Indies. All was for naught, however, as a miscommunication had botched TF-11's reported course. The heavy IJN counterstroke had once again failed to catch the impudent Americans.

The IJN's complete failure to intercept, let alone punish, TF-11 meant that the relatively small February 20, 1942 air–sea clash proved of much greater significance than is generally understood. During the absolute nadir of US naval strength in the Pacific, a single US carrier had brought nearly four times as many combat aircraft to the strike zone as Rabaul could sortie against its attacker. Unbeknownst to the US commanders, *Lexington* had virtually annihilated Rabaul's entire air strength simply by defending herself. Taken to its logical conclusion, the February 20 raid signaled that Japan's entire "outer defensive sphere" Pacific strategy that emphasized counterattacking along interior lines was fatally flawed. Although the IJN high command seemed not to grasp what had just taken place, and US officials had no way of knowing, the resulting implications for Japan's entire Pacific War strategy were ominous indeed.

HALSEY'S TASK FORCE 16 RAIDS WAKE ISLAND, FEBRUARY 24, 1942

By early February 1942 it was clear the Japanese avalanche in Southeast Asia and the East Indies was not slowing. The Japanese had conquered Malaya and were barreling towards Singapore. Additional Japanese forces were descending into Borneo, Celebes, New Guinea, and the Solomons, threatening Allied positions in Sumatra, Java, and Australia. Local Allied defenses were hard-pressed to stem the Japanese tide anywhere, causing the USN to consider additional diversionary attacks on the Japanese perimeter, possibly in the direction of the Home Islands themselves.

On February 11, Nimitz chose to combine Halsey's TF-8 (*Enterprise*) and Fletcher's TF-17 (*Yorktown*) into a single task force of two carrier task groups under Halsey's overall command. Halsey's two-carrier task force would then strike Wake Island, plus Eniwetok Island in the Marshalls; recent submarine reconnaissance had observed little activity at

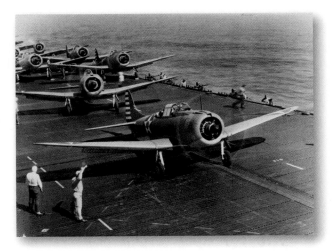

Enterprise Air Group skipper Lieutenant-Commander Howard Young's SBD prepares to launch from *Enterprise*, February 24, 1942. The target is Wake Island, now occupied by the Japanese. Beneath the edge of the flight deck is the antiaircraft gun gallery. (NHHC 80-G-66037)

either base. However, if in Halsey's judgment an attack on Eniwetok was considered inadvisable, it was suggested to Halsey that he might strike Marcus Island instead. The combined two-carrier task force was designated Task Force 13 and was slated to deploy from Pearl Harbor on Friday, February 13.

Perhaps unsurprisingly, this plan immediately disintegrated. Although Halsey's task group had its oiler ready, Fletcher's assigned oiler *Guadalupe* (AO-32) was repeatedly delayed while en route to Pearl Harbor, forcing Fletcher's *Yorktown* group to remain in Pearl Harbor indefinitely until *Guadalupe* arrived. Additionally, Halsey was an old sea dog in touch with the common sailor's sensibilities, and he vigorously protested his task force's new designation and sailing date. Nimitz, "in deference to those who may be superstitious," duly renamed Halsey's *Enterprise* force Task Force 16 and allowed it to sortie just after midnight, February 14.

Task Force 16's mission objectives were:

1. To weaken the enemy and gain information as to his dispositions;
2. To divert enemy strength from his offensives in the southwest;
3. To cover [Allied] positions and communications in the mid-Pacific.

However, if "important enemy combatant forces were encountered within striking distance, these forces would become the prime objective."

Fletcher's TF-17 sortied on February 16, and comprised carrier *Yorktown*, heavy cruisers *Astoria* and *Louisville*, six destroyers, and oiler *Guadalupe*. Nimitz directed Halsey to hit Eniwetok with *Enterprise* just before sunrise, February 24, while Fletcher's *Yorktown* struck Wake Island.

Meanwhile, the Southeast Asia situation continued to deteriorate rapidly, with Singapore falling on February 15. Singapore's collapse may have convinced King that the diversionary strikes were no longer as urgent as they once had been. Additionally, according to a wartime USN combat narrative, "an unofficial report [claimed that] aircraft were vitally needed at this time to guard a large commercial ship which had just put in at Palmyra Island south of Hawaii." Regardless, Fletcher's TF-17 was dismissed from the combined strike, leaving Halsey to complete his mission with TF-16 alone. With only one carrier available, target Eniwetok was scrubbed. Halsey would instead hit Wake with *Enterprise* and a possible surface bombardment.

Halsey's primary targets at Wake would be warships, aircraft, merchantmen, support installations, ground troops and fortifications, and storehouses, in that order. On February 21 Halsey directed *Enterprise* alone to hit Wake, but apparently changed his mind, as he added a simultaneous surface shelling to his orders the next day. Both *Enterprise* and the gunships would hit Wake ten minutes before sunrise on February 24.

Spruance's detachment of heavy cruisers *Northampton* and *Salt Lake City*, plus destroyers *Balch* and *Maury*, detached from TF-16 late on February 23 and proceeded separately through the night. They would hit Wake from the west. Meanwhile, *Enterprise* continued south overnight, escorted by destroyers *Dunlap* (DD-384), *Blue* (DD-387), *Ralph Talbot* (DD-390), and *Craven* (DD-382).

A few days earlier, a B-17 heavy bomber out of Midway had made a photoreconnaissance pass of Wake Island. The resulting photographs were developed at Pearl Harbor and then flown out to *Enterprise* at sea by a PBY.

By 0517hrs, February 24 *Enterprise* was 120nm north of Wake Island and began launching her aircraft. Rain, darkness, and overcast made launch

Early on February 24, *Enterprise* crew observed "a curious effect" from the humidity—contrails forming around the tips of the US planes' propellers, seen here. The phenomenon was apparently rare and fascinating enough to merit its inclusion in after-action reports. (US Navy)

An oblique, low-altitude view of Wake burning during the February 24, 1942 raid by Halsey's Task Force 16. The wreck in the foreground is a Japanese ship sunk by the US garrison during the IJN's December 1941 invasion of the island. (NHHC 80-G-85197)

operations difficult, and one plane and airman were lost on takeoff. *Enterprise*'s strike was 30 minutes late assembling and departing for the target. Four fighters were then launched as TF-16 combat air patrol.

Enterprise's strike came to 36 Dauntlesses, nine Devastators, and six Wildcats for a total of 51 aircraft led by Commander Howard L. Young. Each of the Dauntlesses was armed with one 500lb bomb and two 100lb bombs, while each Devastator carried twelve 100lb bombs. The Dauntlesses and Wildcats flew at 14,000–18,000ft, while the Devastators flew at 12,000ft.

Meanwhile, as dawn approached, Spruance's detached surface ships proceeded in a 1,500-yard column. In the lead was destroyer *Maury*, with cruisers *Northampton* and *Salt Lake City* in the center, and destroyer *Balch* in the rear. While the Spruance group was still 18nm from Wake, three Nakajima E8N2 Dave reconnaissance floatplanes were sighted at 0707hrs, while the ragged *Enterprise* launch meant Spruance's assigned fighter escort was not yet on station. Unmolested, the Japanese floatplanes dive-bombed *Maury* and *Northampton* but missed. At 0742hrs the US ships opened fire on Wake's Peale Island. Range was 16,000 yards.

The *Enterprise* strike reached Wake eight minutes later. Weather over the target was considerably better than at the *Enterprise* launch point, with clear skies and unlimited ceiling. The Dauntlesses commenced dive-bombing the airfield and other shore targets around 0755hrs. With no parked aircraft immediately visible, the SBDs concentrated on the runway, underground shelters, and magazines. Some SBDs dropped all three bombs on the first attack; others made up to three dives.

Simultaneously the TBDs roared in on horizontal bombing runs, with one section attacking the gasoline stowage at Wake's southwest. A second TBD section first bombed an antiaircraft battery on Wilkes Island, before attacking the old Pan American Airways tanks on eastern Wilkes. Several more bombs fell on the old USMC camp. Erratic 3in. and 5in. antiaircraft batteries proved ineffective against the Americans, and *Enterprise*'s VB-6 alone ultimately dumped over six tons of bombs on Wake Island.

As the column leader, destroyer *Maury* was tasked with alerting the rest of the force of enemy scout planes and firing on them. She accordingly expended only 348 5in. rounds at shore targets, all antiaircraft shells. Her partner, destroyer *Balch*, unloaded 995 rounds of 5in. high-explosive shells at shore targets, plus another 199 5in. antiaircraft shells. According to one destroyer officer: "5in. gunfire was again apparently effective in silencing shore batteries of the character installed on these islands."

For the cruisers, *Northampton* expended a total of 264 8in. high-explosive shells, and *Salt Lake*

City added another 261, with ranges between 14,000 and 16,000 yards throughout the bombardment. Unlike the destroyer officers, the cruiser officers were not impressed with these initial US Navy bombardments. According to one: "Firing at [shore batteries] with cruiser 8in. is … wasteful of ammunition for the results obtained." Another officer claimed: "When available, bombardment ammunition should be provided for these operations. With limited expenditures necessitated by the use of armor-piercing projectiles, excellent objectives usually appear late in the bombardment. In this case, an excellent enfilade was afforded on the eastern end of Wake Island which could not be utilized."

Spruance's bombardment force proceeded to the TF-16 rendezvous point 20nm northeast of Wake Island, While en route at 0845hrs, they ran into a 175-ton Japanese patrol boat that *Enterprise* planes had already been attacking. Leading the column, *Maury* opened fire with her 5in. guns and promptly sank it at a range of 3,000 yards. *Maury* then prepared to rescue the Japanese in the water. Almost immediately, a Japanese floatplane, taking advantage of *Maury*'s distracted condition, snuck in and dropped two bombs, missing the destroyer by 50 yards. *Maury* promptly abandoned her humanitarian mission and steamed on.

By 0947hrs both cruisers had recovered all six of their floatplanes, and Spruance's group set off to the northeast at 25 knots. An hour later the US column sighted a 400-ton Japanese patrol boat almost dead ahead at six miles. Within a few minutes *Balch* had sunk it, and by 1130hrs *Balch* had picked up four Japanese survivors. Multiple Japanese floatplanes uneventfully shadowed Spruance's ships the rest of the day. Then suddenly at 1743hrs, two twin-engined bombers cleverly snuck in from a different direction and released their payloads from 13,000ft. Four bombs landed near the two cruisers, causing no damage. Evening fell and Spruance's ships reunited with *Enterprise* and company at 0730hrs the following morning. Halsey's TF-16 retired in the general direction of Midway, diving into the now-familiar "*Enterprise* weather" for concealment.

Heavy cruiser *Salt Lake City* unleashes a shore bombardment during the early 1942 raids. This photograph traditionally has been assumed to be of the February 24 Wake attack. *Salt Lake City* would eventually play a major role in the May 1943 Battle of the Komandorski Islands. (NHHC NH 50946)

Japanese prisoners-of-war from a sunken patrol boat, February 24, 1942. US destroyer *Balch* had recovered the four prisoners after sinking their boat a number of miles off Wake, during Spruance's retirement. An earlier, separate recovery attempt of Japanese survivors from a previous boat had to be aborted when the US ships were bombed. (US Navy)

HALSEY STRIKES MARCUS ISLAND, MARCH 4, 1942

Aboard *Enterprise* the evening of February 25, Halsey received a message from Nimitz: "Desirable to strike Marcus if you think it feasible." A triangular-shaped atoll just a few miles wide, Marcus Island lies 600nm northwest of Wake Island, straddling a straight line running directly from Wake towards southern Japan. Marcus had officially been annexed by the Japanese in 1898, under whom

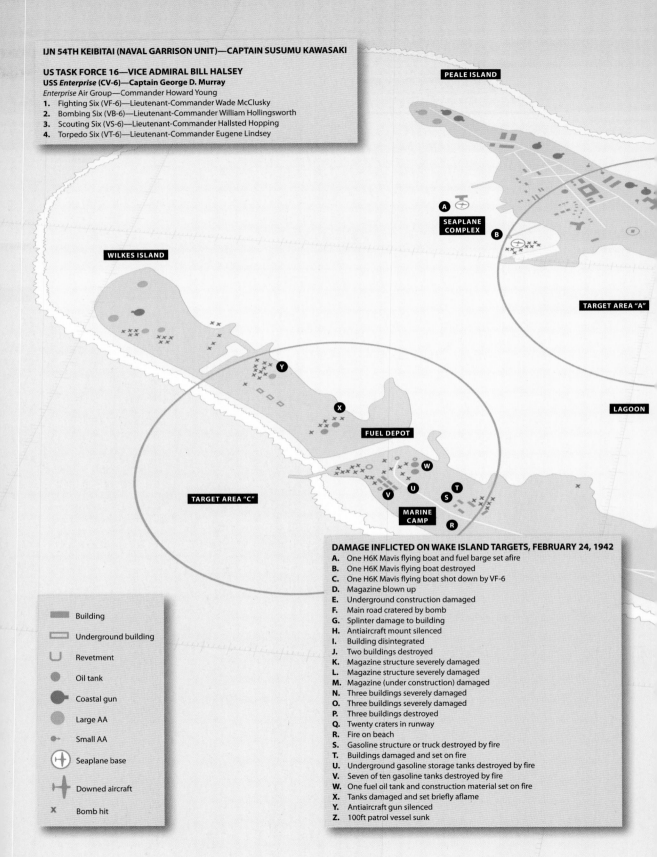

IJN 54TH KEIBITAI (NAVAL GARRISON UNIT)—CAPTAIN SUSUMU KAWASAKI

US TASK FORCE 16—VICE ADMIRAL BILL HALSEY
USS _Enterprise_ (CV-6)—Captain George D. Murray
Enterprise Air Group—Commander Howard Young
1. Fighting Six (VF-6)—Lieutenant-Commander Wade McClusky
2. Bombing Six (VB-6)—Lieutenant-Commander William Hollingsworth
3. Scouting Six (VS-6)—Lieutenant-Commander Hallsted Hopping
4. Torpedo Six (VT-6)—Lieutenant-Commander Eugene Lindsey

PEALE ISLAND

A

SEAPLANE
COMPLEX

B

TARGET AREA "A"

WILKES ISLAND

Y

X

LAGOON

FUEL DEPOT

W

TARGET AREA "C"

V   U   T
        S
MARINE
CAMP
        R

DAMAGE INFLICTED ON WAKE ISLAND TARGETS, FEBRUARY 24, 1942
A. One H6K Mavis flying boat and fuel barge set afire
B. One H6K Mavis flying boat destroyed
C. One H6K Mavis flying boat shot down by VF-6
D. Magazine blown up
E. Underground construction damaged
F. Main road cratered by bomb
G. Splinter damage to building
H. Antiaircraft mount silenced
I. Building disintegrated
J. Two buildings destroyed
K. Magazine structure severely damaged
L. Magazine structure severely damaged
M. Magazine (under construction) damaged
N. Three buildings severely damaged
O. Three buildings severely damaged
P. Three buildings destroyed
Q. Twenty craters in runway
R. Fire on beach
S. Gasoline structure or truck destroyed by fire
T. Buildings damaged and set on fire
U. Underground gasoline storage tanks destroyed by fire
V. Seven of ten gasoline tanks destroyed by fire
W. One fuel oil tank and construction material set on fire
X. Tanks damaged and set briefly aflame
Y. Antiaircraft gun silenced
Z. 100ft patrol vessel sunk

Building

Underground building

Revetment

Oil tank

Coastal gun

Large AA

Small AA

Seaplane base

Downed aircraft

x   Bomb hit

ENTERPRISE RAIDS WAKE ISLAND, FEBRUARY 24, 1942

CONSTRUCTORS' CAMP

C

JAPANESE PATROL BOAT

Z

D

E

F

G

H

I

J

K

WAKE ISLAND

UNDERGROUND HANGARS

L

M

TARGET AREA "B"

Q

A

AGROUND IJN PATROL BOAT. NO. 32 (EX-DESTROYER AOI)

AGROUND IJN PATROL BOAT. NO. 33 (EX-DESTROYER HAGI)

N

P

O

TF-16 raids Marcus and Wake, February 14–March 9, 1942

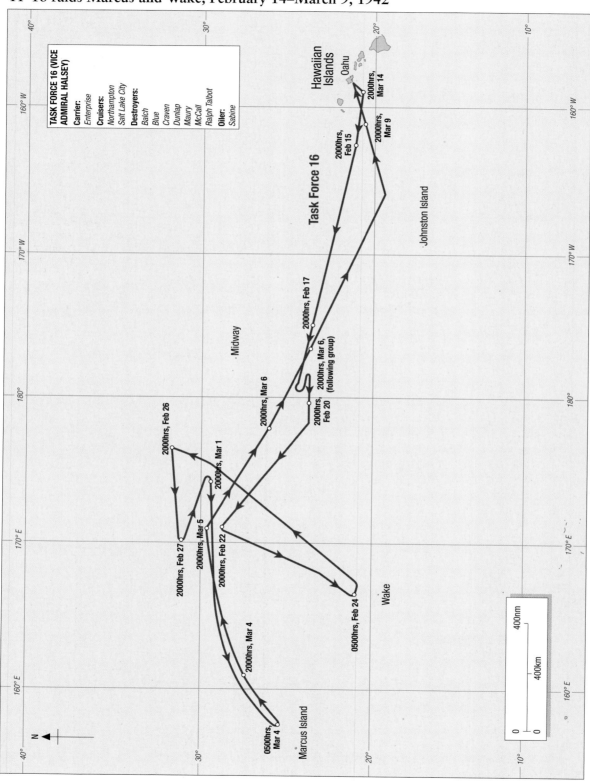

TASK FORCE 16 (VICE ADMIRAL HALSEY)
Carrier:
Enterprise
Cruisers:
Northampton
Salt Lake City
Destroyers:
Balch
Blue
Craven
Dunlap
Maury
McCall
Ralph Talbot
Oiler:
Sabine

Task Force 16

Hawaiian Islands

Oahu

2000hrs, Mar 14

2000hrs, Feb 15

2000hrs, Mar 9

Johnston Island

2000hrs, Feb 17

2000hrs, Mar 6, (following group)

2000hrs, Mar 6

Midway

2000hrs, Feb 20

2000hrs, Feb 26

2000hrs, Feb 27

2000hrs, Mar 1

2000hrs, Mar 5

2000hrs, Feb 22

Wake

0500hrs, Feb 24

2000hrs, Mar 4

0500hrs, Mar 4

Marcus Island

N

400nm

400km

0

0

it was known as Minami-Tori-Shima. Otherwise virtually nothing was known about Marcus, although USN intelligence tentatively believed it was an administrative center with weather and radio facilities.

Official USN charts labeled Marcus as exactly 999nm from Tokyo. "That figure," Halsey recollected, "comprised our knowledge of Marcus, except that it was within easy range of planes from Iwo Jima and was supposed to be well defended. This would be another morale raid. By venturing so near the home islands of the Empire, we would presumably disconcert the Japs and stimulate the Allies more than ever."

A modern view of Marcus Island (Minami-Tori-Shima). A US Coast Guard base was located there until 1993. Tiny Marcus is one of the most isolated islands in the world, a factor inspiring *Enterprise* to lead her aircraft there by radar homing. (Public Domain)

Halsey knew that outnumbered US forces striking so deep into the Empire would require high speed throughout the approach and the withdrawal. Halsey would therefore leave his oiler and fuel-hungry destroyers well behind and rendezvous with them after the attack. On February 28 Halsey ordered *Enterprise* and Spruance's heavy cruisers *Northampton* and *Salt Lake City* to steam for a launch point 175nm northeast of Marcus. Assisted by a full moon during launch and aerial rendezvous operations, *Enterprise* would launch a single unescorted strike, SBDs only, that was timed to hit Marcus before sunrise. Despite having just hit Wake, TF-16's subsequent course of 275 degrees was nearly due west. Halsey recalled, "My staff officers made a point of glancing at the compass from time to time and muttering, 'Two-seven-five … Two-seven-five … Why do we always seem to retire to the westward?'" As he had previously, Halsey successfully exploited heavy storms to make his approach under cover.

Nevertheless, heavy rain on March 2 compelled *Enterprise* to break radio silence to recover her disoriented morning search planes. Then on two separate occasions that same day *Enterprise* patrols would discover and unsuccessfully bomb a surfaced submarine; this turned out to be USS *Gudgeon* (SS-211). The following day, Halsey received amplified intelligence that Marcus might have an airfield, requiring a change in plans. The previously unescorted strike would now have to be accompanied by fighter escort, forcing Halsey to close to within 125nm of Marcus instead of the planned 175nm.

By early morning, March 4 *Enterprise* and her two cruiser escorts were approaching Marcus from the northeast. By 0438hrs the Americans had reached the modified launch point 125nm from the target. Eight minutes later *Enterprise* turned into the wind and began launching her aircraft. Led by *Enterprise* Air Group skipper Commander Howard L. "Brigham" Young, *Enterprise*'s 38-plane strike comprised 32 SBD Dauntless dive-bombers, each armed with one 500lb bomb and two 100lb bombs, plus six F4F Wildcat fighters as escort. By 0504hrs the last plane was aloft, and *Enterprise*, *Northampton*, and *Salt Lake City* immediately turned about, retiring east at 25 knots. A single F4F failed to make the aerial rendezvous and had to abort. Remaining with *Enterprise* were nine F4F fighters to fly CAP and—held in reserve for unexpected naval targets of opportunity—all of Torpedo Six.

Surrounded entirely by ocean for 600nm in every direction, tiny and lonely Marcus was an easy target to miss. Worse, the full moon's expected illumination was largely obscured by a heavy 9/10ths overcast of cumulus clouds at a base 4,000ft altitude. Fortunately a brand-new navigation tactic was being used for the first time: *Enterprise* was guiding her strike into the target via shipboard radar, using voice radio to inform her planes when they drifted off course, and by how much. This was essentially a basic fighter direction tactic, except instead of *Enterprise*'s radar guiding her fighters to an outbound interception, radar was guiding *Enterprise*'s own strike to the target.

The new method was successful. Flying above the overcast, the *Enterprise* strike sighted Marcus "nestling in the moonlight" through a hole in the clouds at 0630hrs. Excellent navigation and a strong tailwind had put the Americans 30 minutes ahead of schedule. Fearing his planes would be heard by the Japanese, Commander Young ordered the attack to proceed immediately. Ideally, the Wildcats would strafe the target first, suppressing Japanese batteries prior to the dive-bombers attacking, but Young's radio transmission failed to reach VF-6 skipper Lieutenant-Commander Wade McClusky.

Meanwhile, assigned to hit Marcus Island's airfield, Bombing Six's 17 SBDs separated into three divisions which closed the island from the south and west. A single SBD detached from the leading section to observe and broadcast information on the target. At 0640hrs the SBDs commenced their attack runs from 16,000ft, plunging through the overcast and dropping parachute flares to illuminate the airfield before dropping their bombs at altitudes of 2,000–3,000ft. Bombing Six's attack lasted five minutes, ending at 0645hrs. Immediately following Bombing Six were the 14 Scouting Six SBDs, whose pilots variously attacked using both conventional dives or shallower-angle glide-bombing approaches begun below the overcast.

As Halsey recalled, "Their radio had just begun to yell when a direct hit knocked it off the air. This brought a plane over from Iwo to investigate, and during our withdrawal we had the satisfaction of hearing it make a report that caused an alert and a black-out in Tokyo."

No Japanese aircraft were sighted at Marcus, either in the air or on the ground, but Marcus was well defended by antiaircraft batteries. In addition to at least three "3in. guns" (one at each corner of the triangular island) a heavy volume of lighter antiaircraft fire was reported from 20mm and 37mm antiaircraft guns. According to a Bombing Six report, these lighter guns proved "much more accurate than any previously encountered and at times came uncomfortably close."

Japanese flak proved severe enough to discourage any subsequent American passes to investigate the damage in detail. Overall the Americans found disappointingly few targets on Marcus. Nevertheless, an apparent fuel storage tank was hit and set on fire, as were several buildings or hangars on both sides of the airfield. Two large fires and a number of smaller fires would still be visible from 20–30nm away.

Marcus Island's persistent antiaircraft fire even followed the *Enterprise* strike out as it retired, the Americans reporting, "Planes retiring when as far as five miles away saw tracers close aboard." The Americans lost a single plane during the strike, a Scouting Six SBD which was observed ditching into the sea ten miles east of Marcus at 0805hrs. Lieutenant Hart Dale Hinton and his gunner were subsequently taken prisoner by the Japanese. By 1000hrs the surviving strike planes had returned to *Enterprise*, which was already high-tailing it hard east at 30 knots accompanied by the escorting *Northampton* and *Salt Lake City*.

The following morning, March 5, found Halsey's three fleeing US warships once more concealed beneath "delightfully ugly" storms, but within hours *Enterprise* and Spruance's cruisers had re-united with their escorting destroyers. All would refuel from oiler *Sabine* (AO-25) on March 6. Favorably wretched weather then returned for another three straight days, by which time TF-16's withdrawal was complete.

The exact amount of damage *Enterprise* had inflicted against Marcus, and the attack's potential significance, remained somewhat uncertain to the Americans. Japanese radio propaganda scoffed merely that the mysterious American carrier raid "had killed eight people and wrecked a shanty." At least one US officer agreed, opining that "the Japs didn't mind [the Wake and Marcus] raids any more than a dog minds a flea."

A more studied CINCPAC observed, "The raid against Marcus caused some concern as to the defenses of the Japanese homeland, but the exact amount of diversion from Japanese effort in the southwest cannot be measured at this time." In fact, "the exact amount of diversion" caused by the American carriers' recent raids was considerably more than Nimitz would have dared believe.

Several US officers and an American news correspondent eat lunch and relax atop *Enterprise*'s island on March 4, 1942. They are awaiting news of the *Enterprise* Air Group's strike on Marcus Island. This was the closest any attacking US ship had yet come to the Home Islands. (NHHC 80-G-66028)

SHOKAKU AND *ZUIKAKU* REDEPLOY TO DEFEND THE HOME ISLANDS

Ordered home for a planned refit, *Shokaku* had departed Truk for the Home Islands on January 30, arriving on February 3. She thus just missed the brief, impromptu attempt by *Akagi*, *Kaga*, and *Zuikaku* to catch the February 1 Marshalls raiders. After the chase was canceled on February 2, *Akagi*, *Kaga*, and *Zuikaku* steamed to Palau, but *Zuikaku* was then reassigned to join her sister in the Home Islands. *Zuikaku* departed Palau on February 9 and arrived at Yokosuka four days later.

Between February 16 and February 28 *Zuikaku* would deploy to Honshu's Mikawa Bay, awaiting possible orders to sortie against any US carriers approaching to attack the Home Islands. Meanwhile, *Shokaku* would only enter drydock at Yokosuka on February 27, a staggering 24 days after arriving home. Whether through administrative failure or simply a lack of urgency, such wartime disorganization contrasted sharply with Nimitz's Pacific Fleet and boded ominously for the IJN's long-term prospects against the USN.

Shokaku would re-emerge from drydock on March 4. Two days later *Zuikaku* departed Kure to intercept Halsey's *Enterprise* task force (TF-16) which had just raided Marcus Island. The following day, March 7, *Zuikaku* was joined by *Shokaku* sortieing out of Yokosuka. Four days later *Shokaku* and *Zuikaku* joined Vice Admiral Shiro Takasu's battleships *Ise* and *Hyuga* in a sweep to intercept US naval forces which were believed to be approaching the Home Islands. After coming up empty, both *Shokaku* and *Zuikaku* returned to Yokosuka on March 16. The following day *Shokaku* and *Zuikaku* would depart Yokosuka to prepare for Nagumo's coming Indian Ocean offensive.

Japanese fleet carrier *Zuikaku* seen just as she entered service in late 1941. *Zuikaku* and her sister *Shokaku* proved the two finest Japanese carriers of the war. They were also the last of the Pearl Harbor veterans to be destroyed, with *Zuikaku* finally sunk in October 1944. (NHHC NH 73067)

In fact, back on March 1, intercepted radio traffic had indicated to US Pacific Fleet intelligence that the IJN 5th Carrier Division, fleet carriers *Shokaku* and *Zuikaku*, were operating in the Bonins area off Japan. For the next two weeks US intelligence feared CarDiv-5 and additional reinforcements were intended for a major offensive into the Central Pacific. The idea that the IJN was seriously worried about an American attack on the Japanese homeland seemed impossible. Only on March 13 would an incredulous Nimitz finally accept that *Shokaku* and *Zuikaku* were engaged in a purely defensive patrol of the Home Islands and were not actually preparing to mount an offensive raid into the Central Pacific.

THE JAPANESE INVASION OF LAE AND SALAMAUA, MARCH 8, 1942

Operation *R*, the invasion of Rabaul, was the furthest southeast that the Japanese had planned to extend during the "First Operational Phase." However, back on January 27 an H6K flying boat of the Yokohama Kokutai had discovered an airfield at Surumi, about 160nm southwest of Rabaul. Three miles from Surumi, at Gasmata, Japanese reconnaissance discovered an additional complex of 20 buildings. The Japanese feared the Allies planned to use the Surumi–Gasmata complex to stage bombing missions against Rabaul.

Therefore, on February 1, Yamamoto ordered Fourth Fleet: "The Surumi area will be invaded as soon as possible and an airbase established." However, Halsey's and Fletcher's Marshalls–Gilberts strikes occurred the same day, and the Surumi invasion was postponed a week. Meanwhile, the 8th Special Base Force readied its Surumi plans. The objective was to "invade the Surumi region as soon as possible and quickly establish an airbase in the area, and suppress the threat of enemy attack while at the same time strengthening … strategic preparedness. Further, to obtain a position of advantage in order to develop an aggressive strategy to blockade the communication route from the United States to the Australian mainland and the various islands of the South Pacific."

Two troopships would transport troops of the Maizuru SNLF as well as additional service troops from Rabaul. They would be supported by one cruiser and five destroyers of the 6th Torpedo Squadron and two cruisers and three destroyers of the 18th Torpedo Squadron, with a seaplane carrier providing air support.

Under heavy rain cover, the IJN invasion force and support group sortied from Rabaul at 0515hrs, February 8, and landed unopposed at Surumi and Gasmata the following morning, February 9. The airfield was immediately improved and fortified, although Allied air raids slightly damaged Japanese shipping on February 10–11. By February 12 an airfield sufficient to handle carrier-based IJN fighters had been established at Surumi, followed by a 170-man SNLF garrison the next day. The remaining invasion force subsequently returned to Rabaul.

OPPOSITE

Rear Admiral Sadamichi Kajioka, commander of IJN Fourth Fleet's Lae–Salamaua invasion force. Kajioka's wartime career was largely mediocre. He had been in command at the first disastrous Wake invasion, but was allowed to lead the second attempt. He later commanded the aborted Port Moresby invasion force. Kajioka died in September 1944 after his destroyer was torpedoed by USS *Growler*. (NHHC NH 101038)

By March 1 the Rabaul area's primary air unit, the 24th Air Flotilla (Koku Sentai), had a strength of 27 A5M4 Claude fighters and 12 A6M2 Zero fighters (4th Kokutai), nine insufficiently trained G4M1 Betty bombers (4th Kokutai), eight H6K4 Mavis flying boats (Yokohama Kokutai), and 18 G3M2 Nell bombers (1st Kokutai).

However, the Australians operated two small fighter strips at Lae and Salamaua in northeastern New Guinea, manned by about 50 to 100 volunteer militia each. About 30nm southwest of Salamaua was a third small airfield at Wau. By using Port Moresby as a relay base and Lae, Salamaua, and Wau as forward bases, the Allies could feasibly stage bombing raids against the Rabaul and Gasmata area from Townsville and Darwin in Australia.

A modern photograph of Lae and the Gulf of Huon taken from a commercial aircraft. Modern Lae has a population of 100,000. The Markham River can be seen flowing into the Gulf of Huon in the center of the picture. (Taro Hama @ e-kamakura via Getty Images)

Therefore, a joint IJA–IJN invasion of the Lae–Salamaua area, codenamed Operation *SR*, was formally agreed to on February 16. According to the plan, on March 3 the IJA South Seas Force would land Major Masao Horie's 2nd Battalion, 144th Infantry Regiment and a mountain artillery company at Salamaua, while an IJN SNLF would come ashore at Lae.

However, the day that the Japanese staffs had gathered at Rabaul to plan the operation—February 20—was the day IJN aerial reconnaissance discovered Brown's *Lexington* task force bearing down on Rabaul from 400nm to the northeast. The subsequent 4th Kokutai attack against Brown's force, described above, so decimated Rabaul-based air strength that the Japanese authorities postponed Operation *SR* five days to March 8.

Rear Admiral Sadamichi Kajioka's Lae–Salamaua Area Invasion Force would comprise light cruiser *Yubari*, seaplane tender *Kiyokawa Maru*, large minelayer *Tsugaru*, destroyers *Oite*, *Yunagi*, *Asanagi*, *Mutsuki*, *Yayoi*, and *Mochizuki*, four minesweepers, and transports *Tenyo Maru*, *Kongo Maru*, *Kokai Maru*, and *Kinryu Maru*. Aboard Kajioka's flotilla was the 8th Base Force of about 620 men. Additionally, to establish the airfield ashore as soon as possible was the 4th Establishment Squad and part-strength 7th Establishment Squad, totaling about 500 service personnel. Boarding IJA transports *Yokohama Maru* and *China Maru* was Major-General Masao Horie's 2nd Battalion, 144th Infantry Regiment.

The *SR* invasion force departed Rabaul at 1300hrs, March 5. IJN seaplane tender *Kiyokawa Maru* provided aerial reconnaissance, while Rear Admiral Eiji Goto's 24th Air Flotilla provided direct air support to the invasion fleet. Escorting the invasion force was Rear Admiral Aritomo Goto's Support Group. The Support Group consisted of the usual 6th and 18th Cruiser divisions comprising heavy cruisers *Aoba*, *Kako*, *Kinugasa*, and *Furutaka*, light cruisers *Tenryu* and *Tatsuta*, and destroyers *Kikuzuki* and *Uzuki*.

At 2100hrs, March 7, the IJN and IJA transport groups divided and proceeded independently towards their respective

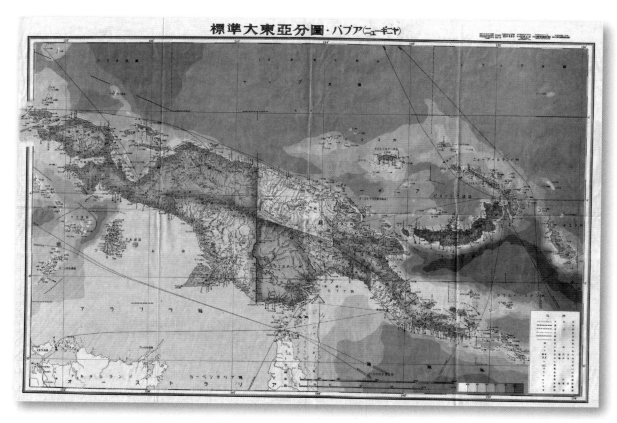

A 1943 Japanese map of Papua New Guinea displays the basic geography of the area as well as the territories occupied by Japanese and Allied forces. New Guinea is the second-largest island in the world, and its highest mountain reaches 16,024ft. New Guinea remains the least-explored area on Earth. (Public Domain)

targets of Lae and Salamaua. The landings themselves were made at night during a severe tropical storm, an impressive feat. The IJN's Kure SNLF came ashore south of Lae at 0230hrs, March 8 and quickly occupied the town and airfield, brushing aside light Australian resistance. Meanwhile, Horie's IJA battalion occupied the Salamaua airfield at 0300hrs. After sunrise, a lone Lockheed Hudson of the RAAF bombed Salamaua, hitting transport *Yokohama Maru* and killing three. The following day an RAAF Hudson attacked Lae, scoring a single hit against destroyer *Asanagi*.

BROWN AND FLETCHER STRIKE LAE AND SALAMAUA, MARCH 10, 1942

After the February 20 action off Bougainville, Vice Admiral Wilson Brown's TF-11 had retired to waters northwest of New Caledonia, where Brown could await further orders in relative safety. After reflecting on TF-11's aborted raid on Rabaul, Brown advised that future carrier raids against major enemy bases be executed with at least two carriers and two oilers, the former to provide sufficient strike power and the latter to provide sufficient operational mobility.

Rabaul was the obvious choice for the war's first twin US carrier strike. On February 25, Leary urged "an early attack" by Brown's suggested two carriers on Rabaul; Leary was particularly concerned about covering a planned US troop convoy from Australia to reinforce Nouméa. With the convoy scheduled for March 7 through March 12, that meant an imminent carrier strike.

Lae–Salamaua, March 10, 1942

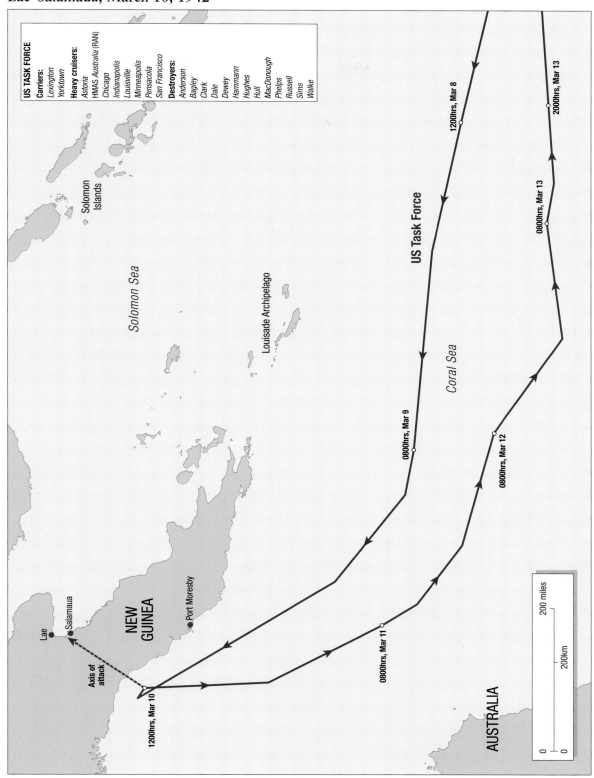

US TASK FORCE

Carriers:
Lexington
Yorktown

Heavy cruisers:
Astoria
HMAS Australia (RAN)
Chicago
Indianapolis
Louisville
Minneapolis
Pensacola
San Francisco

Destroyers:
Anderson
Bagley
Clark
Dale
Dewey
Hammann
Hughes
Hull
MacDonough
Phelps
Russell
Sims
Walke

Solomon Islands

Solomon Sea

Louisade Archipelago

US Task Force

1200hrs, Mar 8

2000hrs, Mar 13

0800hrs, Mar 13

0800hrs, Mar 9

Coral Sea

0800hrs, Mar 12

0800hrs, Mar 11

NEW GUINEA

Port Moresby

Lae

Salamaua

Axis of attack

1200hrs, Mar 10

AUSTRALIA

200 miles
200km

Despite his recommendation a few days previously, Brown apparently had a later date in mind for a dual-carrier raid, radioing Nimitz on February 26 that he did not recommend an immediate carrier strike on Rabaul "under the present conditions." Nevertheless, Nimitz agreed with Leary that the convoy had to be covered, and he had already decided to execute Brown's proposed Rabaul mission.

In fact, Nimitz already had a second carrier task force available. Fletcher's TF-17 had departed Pearl Harbor back on February 17 under orders to deploy as a temporary reserve near the Canton Island area, halfway between Hawaii and Fiji; while Halsey was striking Wake and Marcus with *Enterprise* alone, Fletcher would wait for orders. Under Fletcher were carrier *Yorktown*, heavy cruisers *Astoria* and *Louisville*, six destroyers, and oiler *Guadalupe*.

On February 27 Nimitz ordered Fletcher to proceed to a point 300nm north of Nouméa to rendezvous with Brown's TF-11 at 1200hrs, March 6. Unfortunately, TF-17 had trouble decoding the signal and Fletcher had to send a destroyer to Canton Island to request Pearl Harbor retransmit the message. By the time the destroyer returned, much time had been wasted and TF-17 had to hustle to the rendezvous point at increased speed.

On March 3, with TF-11 approaching the New Hebrides, oiler *Kaskaskia* intercepted TF-11 and began refueling Brown's ships. That same day Brown received orders from King to combine TF-11, TF-17, and the ANZAC Squadron for a two-carrier strike on Rabaul about March 10. Despite the earlier communications foul-up, Fletcher's TF-17 rendezvoused with Brown's TF-11 on time on March 6, suddenly putting Brown in command of two carriers, eight cruisers, and 14 destroyers.

Fletcher and his staff came aboard *Lexington* to confer with Brown and his officers about a plan to attack Rabaul. King's earlier message had suggested attacking Rabaul from the east or southeast, but Brown had tried that approach on February 20 and found the Japanese alert and waiting for him. Brown now preferred attacking from the south, with an added twist from *Lexington*'s Captain Ted Sherman: moonlight strikes against Rabaul and the Gasmata airfield in New Britain. However, *Yorktown*'s air officer Commander Murr Arnold informed Brown that—unlike *Lexington*'s Dauntless and Devastator squadrons—*Yorktown*'s bomber squadrons were not night-qualified. Brown was forced to drop the night attacks and he instead proposed dawn air strikes against Rabaul and Gasmata, potentially followed by opportunistic cruiser bombardments. From Washington, King ordered simply, "Attack enemy."

The towering, jungle-carpeted Owen Stanley Mountains are viewed in this modern photograph by Colin Freeman. *Yorktown* flyers were equipped merely with "a bottle of Aspirin and a machete" in the event their plane went down here, a truly frightening prospect. (CC BY 3.0)

However, late on March 7 Leary forwarded a disturbing report to Brown: an RAAF patrol plane had sighted a major convoy steaming off northeastern New Guinea, while that same day, separate aerial reconnaissance had observed 23 ships in Rabaul. Hard confirmation of a major Japanese operation was received the next morning, March 8, when it was reported that Japanese forces had landed at Lae and Salamaua on New Guinea and seized airfields at both locations.

The Japanese had supposedly debarked from 11 ships, and the March 8 air reconnaissance over Rabaul found the harbor virtually empty; Gasmata, too, was discovered to have "virtually no worthwhile targets."

Additionally, several unexpected foul-ups on March 8 had forced Brown's task force to break radio silence. Not only was Rabaul mostly empty, but Brown now had to assume its defenders were waiting for him. Moreover, the Japanese had once again seized the initiative with the unexpected Lae–Salamaua offensive.

However, Brown's operations officer, Captain Turner Joy, called the development an "answer to prayer." Although the Japanese invasion force had not been sunk in harbor or in transit, the landings themselves were in their most vulnerable phase. Still attempting to consolidate, troops would be disorganized and unfortified ashore, while for several days ships would be stuck on the beach unloading. For the first time in the Pacific War, a strong US force found itself in position to disrupt a Japanese landing. Brown therefore canceled the Rabaul strike and made plans to hit Lae and Salamaua instead.

SBD-3 Dauntless dive-bombers from *Yorktown* en route to their targets at the Gulf of Huon on March 10, 1942. They are flying at an altitude of 14,000ft. Unlike the TBDs, the dive-bombers had no problem surmounting the high mountains of Papua New Guinea. (NHHC NH 95437)

To strike Lae and Salamaua, Brown had two general options. The first and most obvious was the "front door": Brown could round Papua to the north, penetrate the Bismarck Sea, and launch from the northern or seaward side, facing Lae and Salamaua on the Huon Gulf. However, Brown's only Bismarck Sea charts relied on dubious French surveys from the 1700s.

The second option, which Brown ultimately selected, was the "back door": the US carriers would approach from the south, through the Coral Sea, and fly their planes over New Guinea's towering 13,248ft Owen Stanley mountain range to strike Lae and Salamaua from the landward side. However, the formidable Owen Stanleys made for dangerous navigation—the mountains are high and steep, are often smothered in thick weather and high clouds, and are covered in dense, monotonous jungle that lacks any settlements or tracks to function as navigational landmarks. Brown later explained his reasoning:

1.   Experience of February 20 had shown that the enemy was maintaining an extensive search to the eastward of Rabaul.

2.   Greater mutual protection would be afforded by keeping all units together, and better control of movement and timing of attack effected.

3.   Advance from the south offered a shorter route to the selected objectives, involving less expenditure of fuel and consequently affording more fuel for high speed.

4.   There was more likelihood of encountering a southeast wind, which would facilitate retirement after the attack.

Leary had additionally put Rear Admiral John Crace's ANZAC Squadron of four cruisers and four destroyers at Brown's disposal. Under Crace were heavy cruisers *Astoria*, *Chicago*, *Louisville*, and HMAS *Australia*, plus destroyers *Anderson* (DD-411), *Sims* (DD-409), *Hammann* (DD-412), and *Hughes* (DD-410). Brown subsequently ordered the reluctant Crace to take his squadron south of Rossel Island as distant cover to Port Moresby and New Caledonia; Crace would additionally escort Brown's two oilers to the

Yorktown TBD torpedo-bombers of VT-5 fly over the Gulf of Huon, where Japanese ships can be seen off Salamaua. The distinctively bright livery of early 1942 US aircraft is noticeable on the TBD in the upper right. (NHHC NH 95442)

Japanese seaplane tender *Kiyokawa Maru* maneuvers while under attack from bomb-armed *Yorktown* TBDs, March 10, 1942. *Kiyokawa Maru* and her escorting destroyer were several miles east of the rest of the Japanese force, but they did not escape the Americans' notice. (NHHC NH 95444)

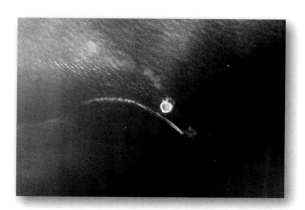

post-strike fueling rendezvous. Although grumbling about "chaperon[ing] a blooming oiler" Crace complied, ruing a seeming missed opportunity to "shoot Japs." Crace's mission would leave just four cruisers and nine destroyers to escort *Lexington* and *Yorktown*.

Lexington's Captain Ted Sherman would plan the combined *Lexington–Yorktown* strike. On March 9 Brown's combined task force headed west towards the scheduled launch point across the Coral Sea. Seeking greater information on flying conditions through the Owen Stanley Mountains, that same day two of Sherman's officers— *Lexington* Air Group skipper Commander Bill Ault and Sherman's staff officer Commander Walton W. Smith—were dispatched in separate SBDs. Smith flew to Townsville in northeastern Australia and Ault flew to Port Moresby in New Guinea, with Ault arriving in between Japanese air raids.

Within a few hours Ault and Smith had safely returned to *Lexington* bearing encouraging information. Based on Ault's and Smith's intelligence, Sherman's staff found a 7,500ft mountain pass for the US strike to fly through. Although usually covered by thick clouds, this particular pass often cleared during the morning for a few hours. Sherman accordingly set the launch time for 0700hrs, March 10.

Worried over the F4F-3 fighters' short range, some thought was given to having the Wildcats quickly land and refuel at Port Moresby, but there was the obvious danger of Japanese bombers catching them on the ground. The other problem was the Devastators. Sherman badly wanted to send at least some TBDs armed with torpedoes to inflict the most possible damage on Japanese shipping, but strike planners were uncertain whether the Devastators could lug the 2,216lb Mark 13 torpedoes over the 7,500ft pass. Both gambling and hedging his bets, Sherman chose to send *Lexington*'s VT-2 armed with torpedoes, and *Yorktown*'s VT-5 armed with two 500lb bombs each.

By dawn, March 10, Brown's combined carrier task force had penetrated the Gulf of Papua and closed to within 45nm of the southern Papua coast. At 0704hrs *Yorktown* launched four Wildcats as CAP. Then, as planned, *Lexington* launched her strike first. Eight VF-3 fighter escorts under Lieutenant-Commander Jimmy Thach took off first, clearing the deck for the 30 SBD Dauntlesses of VS-2 and VB-2, followed by the 13 torpedo-armed TBD Devastators of VT-2. The bombers then headed to the target, while Thach's eight Wildcat fighters landed and topped off their tanks before relaunching; the refueled fighters would easily overtake the bombers before reaching the target.

Then, beginning at 0805hrs, *Yorktown* launched her strike of 30 SBDs, 12 bomb-armed TBDs, and 10 F4Fs as fighter escort. With her more efficient elevators, *Yorktown*'s strike was able to more quickly assemble and depart for the target, without her fighters having to refuel. Each carrier had launched 52 aircraft, for a total of 61 SBDs, 25 TBDs, and 18 F4Fs headed to the target. Thirteen F4Fs and nine SBDs remained behind to defend the combined task force.

Lexington's strike group proceeded ahead of *Yorktown*'s. Upon reaching the designated mountain pass, strike leader Commander Bill Ault pulled away from the formation to observe the weather conditions. Ault decided the weather was adequate and ordered the strike to proceed. His Dauntless unburdened by a bomb, Ault would orbit over the pass throughout the strike, continuously transmitting meteorological conditions to his fellow raiders; once the strike was returning, Ault would meet his charges and shepherd them back through the pass. *Lexington*'s leading Dauntlesses had reached an altitude of 16,000ft, easily summiting the 7,500ft pass. They continued on towards Lae and Salamaua on the Huon Gulf 45nm ahead.

Meanwhile, *Yorktown*'s eight fighter escorts under Thach caught up with *Lexington*'s torpedo-armed Devastators as both squadrons approached the pass. VT-2 commander Lieutenant-Commander Jimmy Brett feared they would have to abort, as his struggling Devastators could not climb as quickly as the mountains were rising beneath them. However, Brett, a former glider pilot, found a relatively flat, sunlit area and flew over it. His intuition was rewarded, as a 1,200ft-per-minute updraft caught the Devastators and just lifted them over the mountains. "Halfway house," Brett called in satisfaction.

With Brett's torpedo-bombers safe, Thach's fighters overtook first them and then the dive-bombers. At 0920hrs the Wildcats were over the strike zone. No Japanese aircraft were visible, either in the sky or on the Salamaua airstrip. Thach split his fighters into two groups, sending one to Lae in the north, while he led a group south to bomb and strafe. In fact, the Japanese had gotten Lae's airfield ready to receive planes the previous evening, and the 24th Air Flotilla was planning to transfer fighters there within hours. But on the morning of March 10 the airfields were still empty.

Huon Gulf hosted 16 Japanese transports, warships, and auxiliaries when the US strike arrived that morning. *Lexington*'s 18 SBDs of VS-2 opened the attack at 0922hrs. Sighting three large transports off Lae from 16,000ft, Lieutenant-Commander Robert Dixon ordered his SBDs to bomb all three. After being pounded by 500lb bombs, *Kongo Maru* was sunk at the Lae docks, *Tenyo Maru* was sunk while anchored in the Gulf, and *Kokai Maru* was left burning. Two of Dixon's SBDs had to pull out of their initial dives when their sights fogged up. They spotted Kajioka's flagship, light cruiser *Yubari*, making steam and struck her with a 500lb bomb, leaving her ablaze.

After antiaircraft fire from 8cm shore batteries shot down a VS-2 SBD, four F4F fighters bombed and strafed them into silence. After shooting up the Lae airfield, the VF-2 fighters made repeated low-level strafing runs against light cruiser *Yubari*, a destroyer, and a minesweeper; by late morning Kajioka's flagship would suffer nine killed and 50 wounded.

As VB-2 and VT-2 arrived, they split up to go after multiple targets. Two near-misses from 1,000lb bombs lightly damaged large minelayer *Tsugaru*. In Salamaua's harbor transport *China*

A *Yorktown* SBD views Japanese auxiliary cruiser *Kongo Maru* sinking off Lae during the Gulf of Huon strike. *Kongo Maru* entered service in 1935 and participated in the Wake and Rabaul invasions before meeting her end here in 1942. (NHHC NH 95434)

US CARRIER RAID AGAINST LAE–SALAMAUA MARCH 10, 1942

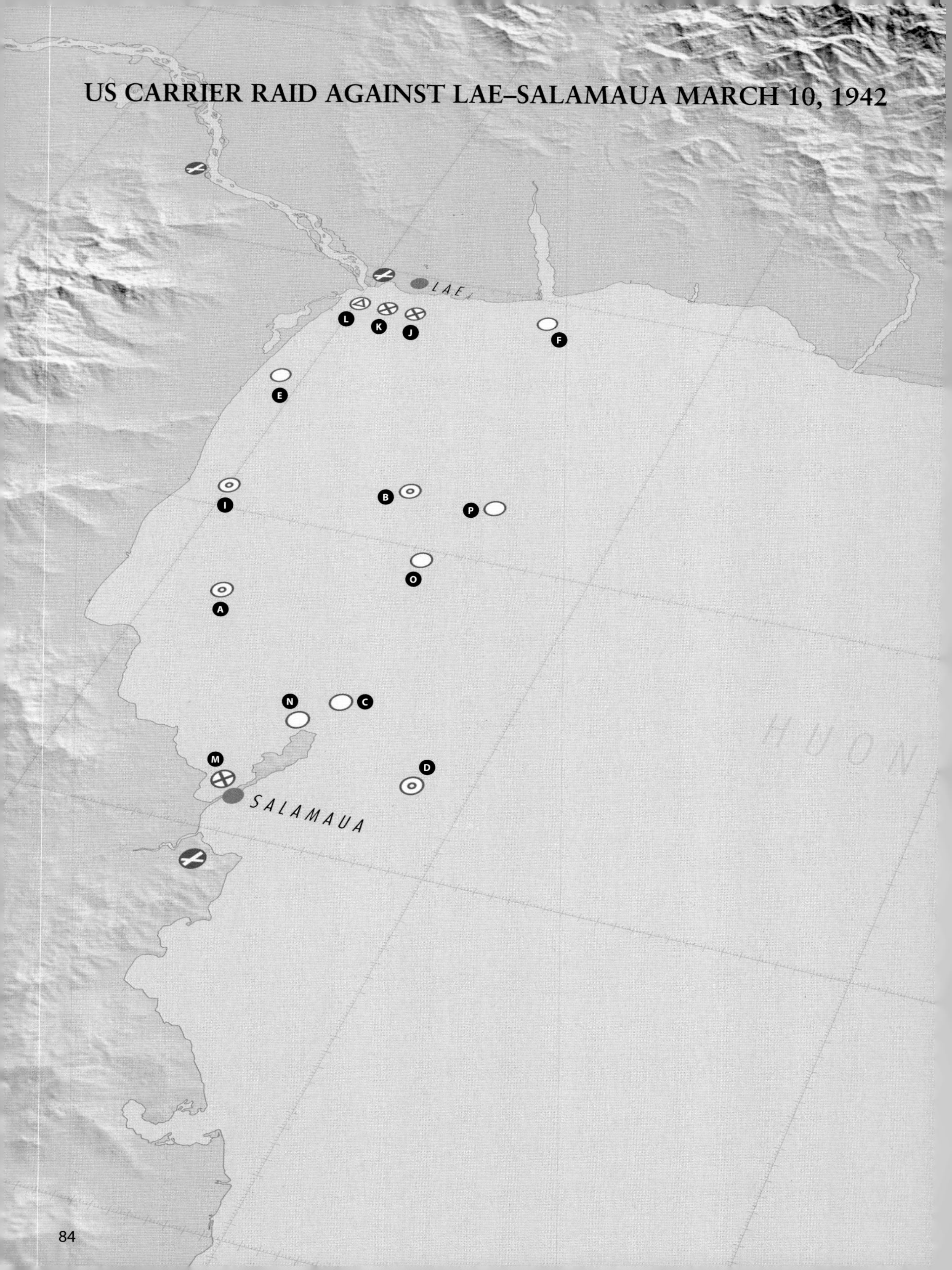

LAE

SALAMAUA

HUON

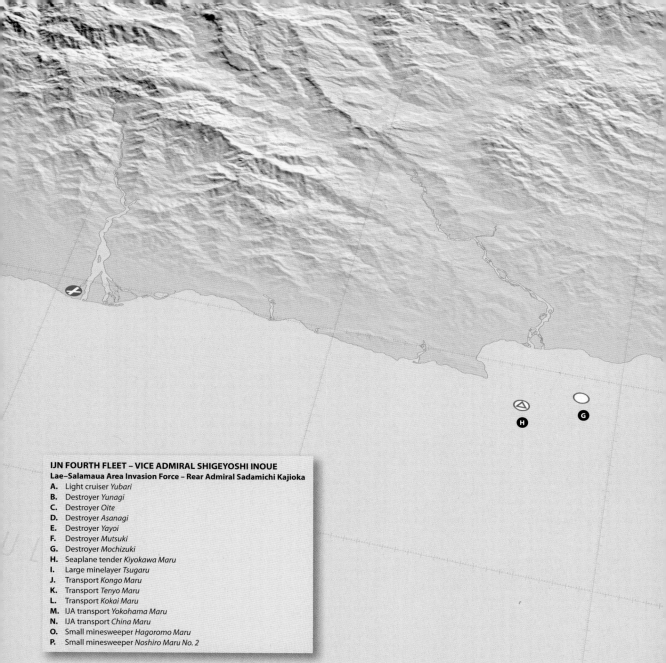

IJN FOURTH FLEET – VICE ADMIRAL SHIGEYOSHI INOUE
Lae–Salamaua Area Invasion Force – Rear Admiral Sadamichi Kajioka

A. Light cruiser *Yubari*
B. Destroyer *Yunagi*
C. Destroyer *Oite*
D. Destroyer *Asanagi*
E. Destroyer *Yayoi*
F. Destroyer *Mutsuki*
G. Destroyer *Mochizuki*
H. Seaplane tender *Kiyokawa Maru*
I. Large minelayer *Tsugaru*
J. Transport *Kongo Maru*
K. Transport *Tenyo Maru*
L. Transport *Kokai Maru*
M. IJA transport *Yokohama Maru*
N. IJA transport *China Maru*
O. Small minesweeper *Hagoromo Maru*
P. Small minesweeper *Noshiro Maru No. 2*

UNITED STATES – VICE ADMIRAL WILSON BROWN
Task Force 11 – Brown
Lexington (CV-2) – Captain Frederick "Ted" Sherman
Lexington Air Group – Commander Bill Ault
    Fighting Three (VF-3) – Lieutenant-Commander Jimmy Thach
    Bombing Two (VB-2) – Lieutenant-Commander Weldon Hamilton
    Scouting Two (VS-2) – Lieutenant-Commander Robert Dixon
    Torpedo Two (VT-2) – Lieutenant-Commander Jimmy Brett
Task Force 17 – Rear Admiral Frank Fletcher
Yorktown (CV-5) – Captain Elliott Buckmaster
Yorktown Air Group – Commander Curtis Smiley
    Fighting Forty-two (VF-42) – Lieutenant-Commander Oscar Pederson
    Bombing Five (VB-5) – Lieutenant-Commander Robert G. Armstrong
    Scouting Five (VS-5) – Lieutenant-Commander William O. Burch
    Torpedo Five (VT-5) – Lieutenant-Commander Joe Taylor

✈	Airfield
◯	Undamaged ship
◉	Light-damaged ship
△	Medium-damaged ship
⊗	Sunk ship

YOKOHAMA MARU COMES UNDER TBD DEVASTATOR ATTACK AT SALAMAUA, MARCH 10, 1942 (PP.86–87)

On Salamaua, having landed troops and unloaded cargo on March 8, 1942, the Japanese troop transport ship *Yokohama Maru* was attacked by an American-built Lockheed Hudson light bomber of the RAAF's No. 32 Squadron based at Port Moresby, New Guinea; she was hit and damaged by one bomb. Two days later, on March 10, the Japanese invasion force was attacked by Vice Admiral Wilson Brown's TF-11, including ships of Rear Admiral Frank J.Fletcher's TF-17. Some 104 aircraft (SBDs, TBDs, and F4Fs) of USS *Lexington* (CV-2) and USS *Yorktown* (CV-5) from the Coral Sea flew over New Guinea's Owen Stanley mountain range to make the attack.

In this scene, around 1000hrs in the morning of the 10th, a TBD Devastator (**1**) from *Lexington*'s VT-2 squadron is making a torpedo run at the *Yokohama Maru* (**2**) in the tight Salamaua Harbor. The TBD Devastator is only flying about 50–75ft off the water, because if it drops the Mark 13 torpedo (**3**) from any higher, the torpedo will malfunction. Moderate Japanese antiaircraft fire is emanating from the *Yokohama Maru* and from the hills nearby, where the Japanese have set up antiaircraft guns. *Yokohama Maru* is shortly to become the first ever victim of the Mark 13 torpedo.

Maru escaped VB-2 unscathed, but nearby *Yokohama Maru* was hit by a TBD's torpedo and sunk. Assisting the bombers at Salamaua were Lieutenant-Commander Jimmy Thach's four F4F fighters, which flew into Japanese flak to strafe enemy gun positions ashore. A single Japanese plane got airborne during the *Lexington* strike. Despite flying a completely outclassed E8N2 Dave floatplane, the Japanese crew aggressively counterattacked the Americans until finally being shot down by a Wildcat in the midst of a *Yubari* strafing run.

The *Yorktown* strike shortly appeared, preceded by *Yorktown* VF-42 fighters which strafed the Lae airfield and small craft in Salamaua Harbor. At 0950hrs 17 SBDs of VB-5 opened attacks against *Yubari* and other fleeing vessels in the Huon Gulf. They were followed 15 minutes later by SBDs of VS-5, which began dive-bombing the transports off Lae. VT-5's bomb-armed TBDs appeared at 1020hrs and made horizontal bombing runs against seaplane tender *Kiyokawa Maru*, which was being escorted by destroyer *Mochizuki* some 25nm east of Lae. Dropping 500lb bombs from 14,000ft, they claimed at least one bomb hit on *Kiyokawa Maru*. Once again the tender scrambled an E8N2 floatplane, which scored insignificant damage on multiple TBDs, and then disappeared.

Shortly after the *Yorktown* TBDs had departed, eight B-17E Flying Fortresses of the USAAF 19th Bombardment Group arrived from Townsville, Australia. This was the second part of Leary's and Brown's land-based strike coordinated with the US carriers. The B-17s were quickly followed by eight Hudson bombers of the RAAF No. 32 Squadron, flying out of Port Moresby. The 16 air force bombers claimed multiple hits on Japanese ships in harbor, although these are not as well documented as the USN strike.

Out of 104 US carrier planes that attacked Lae and Salamaua on March 10, only a single SBD had been lost, to shore-based antiaircraft fire. However, the performance of the Mark 13 torpedoes proved ominous indeed—out of 13 dropped, only one certain hit was observed, despite later analysis suggesting at least nine should have scored.

The March 10 strikes on Lae and Salamaua cost the Japanese a total of 132 killed (126 IJN and six IJA) plus 257 wounded (240 IJN plus 17 IJA). The US carrier strike had sunk large transports *Kongo Maru*, *Tenyo Maru*, and *Yokohama Maru*. Transport *Kokai Maru* and seaplane tender *Kiyokawa Maru* had suffered what Japanese records called "medium damage," while light damage had been inflicted on light cruiser *Yubari*, minelayer *Tsugaru*, destroyers *Asanagi* and *Yunagi*, and minesweeper *Tama Maru*.

Brown began recovering his strike at 1050hrs, and barely an hour later both US carriers were retiring southeastwards at 20 knots. An hour after that, a total of 11 Japanese fighters, delayed by communications issues, began arriving at Lae–Salamaua. Late that afternoon a Yokohama Kokutai H6K4 Mavis sighted *Lexington*'s fleeing TF-11 and radioed a contact report back to Rabaul, but bad weather and the fast-approaching evening prevented a Japanese counterattack. By February 14 Brown's carriers had reunited with their oilers and Crace's cruiser squadron.

Armed with bombs, *Yorktown* TBDs attack Japanese shipping in the Huon Gulf, March 10, 1942. Japanese auxiliary ship *Noshiro Maru* and minesweeper *Hagoromo Maru* can be seen making smoke, in an attempt to foil the American attackers. (Public Domain)

AFTERMATH

While hardly approaching the Pearl Harbor attack, the unexpected Lae–Salamaua raid had shocked Inoue and other IJN officers. Except for the first Wake landing, the IJN had persistently reaped dazzling rewards operating under the principle of economy of force. The USN's Lae–Salamaua raid signaled that these days were over. *Lexington* and *Yorktown* had sunk or damaged 13 of the 18 Japanese ships involved in the landings, dealing the IJN its worst material losses of the Pacific War to date. Inoue was forced to postpone his Tulagi and Port Moresby landings from April to May, setting off a chain of strategic events that in June would prove disastrous at Midway.

Although American historiography always categorizes it separately, the April 18, 1942 Doolittle Raid can rightfully be considered the last and greatest of the early 1942 Pacific carrier raids; all subsequent US fleet carrier operations were either pitched battles or sustained offensives.[3]

The largely overlooked first South Pacific campaign detailed here—that of early 1942—ended abruptly with Coral Sea and Midway. As for the Central Pacific, in mid-1942 US authorities canceled the proposed Operation *Buzzer*, ending any US plans to recapture Wake. The Americans would instead bypass Wake, causing its Japanese garrison to slowly starve. Beginning in 1943 and continuing through the end of the war, increasingly powerful US air and sea forces would chronically abuse Wake *en passant* as a sort of semi-official live target training location, relentlessly pummeling the hapless Japanese outpost so many times by 1945 that no official bombardment count was ever attempted.

The US Pacific Fleet's major naval counteroffensives began in August 1942 (Solomons) and November 1943 (Gilberts). After the Gilberts' Majuro and Kwajalein were taken, they were converted into airbases for land-based US aircraft, including heavy bombers. From here the remaining Japanese islands in the Marshalls and Gilberts were kept suppressed through the end of the war via repeated air attacks; the inspired American strategy of seizing just one or two Japanese-occupied islands in an entire island chain (and then daily bombing and starving the remaining islands into impotence) was not only completely unanticipated by Japanese prewar plans, but largely improvised by the Americans as well.

Those Japanese-occupied Marshall islands that were bypassed were ultimately subjected to 15,289 tons of Allied bombs; Wotje received the most at 4,087 tons. The bypassed Japanese outposts began to starve; by 1945

---

3 For further, detailed reading of the Doolittle operation, the author suggests Osprey Publishing's Campaign series treatment *The Doolittle Raid 1942* by Clayton K.S. Chun.

barely one-third of some Marshall garrison complements remained alive. The greatest leapfrog, however, was in the South Pacific; by August 1945 over 69,000 Japanese troops were marooned at Rabaul, famished and powerless to affect the American advance or even get home.

Perhaps most importantly, in just three months the US Pacific Fleet and especially its carriers had drastically increased their operational competence since the December 1941 Wake disaster. In a strategic sense, the seemingly minor US carrier raids of early 1942 were Yamamoto's and Genda's worst nightmare come true. By opening war with the United States without simultaneously crippling its carrier fleet, the IJN's two carrier masterminds had constructed a self-fulfilling crisis that would ultimately culminate at the disastrous Battle of Midway.

An SBD Dauntless from the new *Yorktown* (CV-10) flies over Wake Island on October 5 or 6, 1943. These 1943 raids helped shape new American tactics before the real hammer blows began to fall on the Japanese perimeter in November 1943. (US Navy)

THE BATTLEFIELDS TODAY

The Japanese garrison at Wake, now under IJN Captain Shigematsu Sakaibara, surrendered on September 4, 1945. In 1947 Sakaibara was put to death for his October 5, 1943 execution of the 98 American prisoners remaining on Wake. The island returned to its prewar status as a US territory and is now occupied by the United States Air Force.

The United States returned Marcus Island (Minami-Tori-Shima) to Japan in 1968. Like Wake, Marcus Island has no permanent population but is manned by military and government personnel of its occupying country.

In 1947, the United Nations officially awarded Japan's former South Seas Mandate to United States trusteeship as the "Trust Territory of the Pacific Islands" (TTPI). The irony barely merits mentioning but has never been lost on the islands' native inhabitants.

The Marianas' Saipan and Tinian voted in 1978 to become the "Commonwealth of the Northern Mariana Islands" (CNMI) under limited US rule. Guam natives, who had been American since 1898, proved understandably bitter over Saipan and Tinian's assistance of the brutal wartime Japanese occupation. Despite sharing a common cultural heritage, in 1969 Guam rejected a referendum to reunify with Saipan and Tinian. Guam remains a US commonwealth separate from the Northern Mariana Islands.

A 5in. gun from the sunken *Lexington* is seen in this remarkable 2018 photograph. *Lexington* was scuttled at the Battle of the Coral Sea on May 8, 1942. She was discovered by Paul Allen's team on March 4, 2018 at a depth of 9,800ft. (COURTESY OF PAUL G. ALLEN; DOUGLAS CURRAN/AFP via Getty Images)

As of 2022 the remaining islands of Japan's South Seas Mandates exist as three nominally independent sovereign nations: the Federated States of Micronesia (FSM), the Republic of the Marshall Islands (RMI), and the Republic of Palau. After decades of negotiation, self-government was achieved for all in 1979, with Micronesia and the Marshall Islands being awarded official independence in 1986 and Palau in 1994. However, all three nations remain under what appears to be permanent American suzerainty as part of a so-called "Compact of Free Association with the United States." What this means is that although the three military-less micronations are officially sovereign and self-ruling, the United States controls their foreign affairs and provides their defense while also providing federal US funds as social assistance. The arrangement's immense national security advantage to both parties is obvious, while the corresponding social and economic advantages to the native islanders is perhaps less so. With their tiny, vastly dispersed populations completely dominated by the United States, it has been fairly observed that these three polities remain, arguably, the most politically insignificant nation-states on Earth.

After 1945 Rabaul was reclaimed by Australia. All of Papua New Guinea, including Rabaul, became independent in 1975. Although surrounded by active volcanoes, Rabaul today is a thriving tourist community because of its geography and history. Lae and Salamaua were retaken by Allied forces in September 1943. Like Rabaul they are now part of the independent state of Papua New Guinea.

Kwajalein has been a major US military base since its 1944 conquest by the United States. It has been used for atomic bomb tests, which claimed its most famous shipwreck, ex-German heavy cruiser *Prinz Eugen*. It has subsequently been a major US missile base. This 1980s photo captures eight multiple independent re-entry vehicles (MIRVs) descending from a single LGM-118A Peacekeeper ballistic missile test. The missile had been launched from California. (Public Domain)

ACRONYMS AND ABBREVIATIONS

A5M Claude	Mitsubishi Navy Type 96 carrier-based fighter	F4F	Grumman F4F Wildcat carrier-based fighter aircraft
A6M Zero	Mitsubishi Type O carrier fighter	FDO	Fighter Direction Officer
AE	ammunition ship (hull classification)	G4M Betty	Mitsubishi Navy Type 1 medium bomber
AMM3/C	Aviation Machinist's Mate 3rd Class	H6K Mavis	Kawanishi Type 97 large flying boat
AN	net-layer (hull classification)	IFF	Identification Friend or Foe
ANZAC	Australian and New Zealand Army Corps	IGHQ	Imperial General Headquarters (Japanese high command)
AO	fleet oiler (hull classification)	IJA	Imperial Japanese Army
AV	seaplane tender (hull classification)	IJAAF	Imperial Japanese Army Air Force
CA	cruiser (hull classification)	IJN	Imperial Japanese Navy
CAG	carrier air group	IJNAF	Imperial Japanese Navy Air Force
CAP	combat air patrol	MF	Medium Frequency
CarDiv	Carrier Division	NGS	Naval General Staff
CIC	Combat Information Center	nm	nautical miles
CINCPAC	Commander-in-Chief Pacific Fleet	PC	patrol craft
COMDESPAC	Destroyer Force, United States Pacific Fleet	PG	patrol gunboat
		PM	patrol monitor
COMINCH	Commander-in-Chief, US Fleet	SBD Dauntless	Douglas SBD Dauntless dive-bomber
CNO	Chief of Naval Operations	SNLF	Special Naval Landing Force
DD	destroyer (hull classification)	SS	submarine (hull classification)
DE	destroyer escort (hull classification)	TBD Devastator	Douglas TBD Devastator torpedo-bomber
DesDiv	Destroyer Division		
E8N Dave	Nakajima Type 95 reconnaissance seaplane		

SELECT BIBLIOGRAPHY

Adcock, Al, *US Heavy Cruisers in Action, Part 1*, Squadron-Signal Publications (2001)

Belote, James H. and Belote, William M., *Titans of the Seas: The Development and Operations of Japanese and American Carrier Task Forces during World War II*, Harper & Row, Publishers Inc. (1975)

Bôeichô Bôei Kenshûjo Senshishitsu (ed), *Senshi sôsho: Minami Taiheiyô Rikugun sakusen <1> Pôto Moresubi–Gashima shoko sakusen* (War history series: South Pacific area army operations (1), Port Moresby–Guadalcanal first campaigns; trans. Dr Steven Bullard), Asagumo Shinbunsha, Tokyo (1968)

Buell, Thomas B., *The Quiet Warrior: A Biography of Admiral Raymond A. Spruance*, Little, Brown, and Company, New York (1974)

Coyle, Brendan, *War on Our Doorstep: The Unknown Campaign on North America's West Coast*, Heritage House Publishing Company, Limited, Surrey, British Columbia (2002)

Evans, David C. and Peattie, Mark R., *Kaigun: Strategy, Tactics, and Technology in the Imperial Japanese Navy 1187–1941*, Naval Institute Press, Annapolis (1997)

Fuchida, Mitsuo and Okumiya, Masatake, *Midway: The Battle that Doomed Japan*, United States Naval Institute, Annapolis (1955)

Halsey, William F., *Admiral Halsey's Story*, McGraw Hill Book Company, New York (1947)

Herder, Brian Lane, *World War II US Fast Carrier Task Force Tactics 1943-45*, Osprey Publishing Ltd., Oxford (2019)

Lundstrom, John B., *The First Team: Pacific Naval Air Combat from Pearl Harbor to Midway*, Naval Institute Press, Annapolis (1984)

Lundstrom, John B., *Black Shoe Carrier Admiral: Frank Jack Fletcher at Coral Sea, Midway, and Guadalcanal*, Naval Institute Press, Annapolis (2006)

Lundstrom, John B., *The First South Pacific Campaign: Pacific Fleet Strategy December 1941 June 1942*, Naval Institute Press, Annapolis (2014)

Office of Naval Intelligence, *Combat Narratives. Early Raids in the Pacific Ocean: February 1 to March 10, 1942*, Suitland (2017)

Prados, John, *Combined Fleet Decoded: The Secret History of American Intelligence and the Japanese Navy in World War II*, Random House Inc., New York (1995)

Morison, Samuel Eliot, *Rising Sun in the Pacific 1931–April 1942*, Naval Institute Press, Annapolis (2010)

Ugaki, Matome, *Fading Victory: The Diary of Admiral Matome Ugaki 1941–1945*, Naval Institute Press, Annapolis (2008)

US Navy, *Enterprise Action Reports* (various, 1942)

Zimm, Alan, "American Calculations of Battleline Strength, 1941–42," in *The Northern Mariner/le marin du nord*, XIX No. 3, (July 2009), pp. 291–317

Websites

http://ajrp.awm.gov.au/

http://pwencycl.kgbudge.com

http://www.combinedfleet.com/

http://www.cv6.org/

https://warfare.gq/dutcheastindies/rabkav.html

https://www.history.navy.mil

https://www.pacificwar.org/au/

www.navsource.org

www.niehorster.org

INDEX

Figures in **bold** refer to illustrations, captions and plates.